HOW TO READ
LONDON

A crash course in London architecture

Chris Rogers

IVY PRESS

First published in the UK in 2017 by
Ivy Press
An imprint of The Quarto Group
The Old Brewery, 6 Blundell Street
London N7 9BH, United Kingdom
T (0)20 7700 6700 F (0)20 7700 8066
www.QuartoKnows.com

© 2017 Quarto Publishing plc

Front cover image (right): Shutterstock/
Vladislav Gajic.

British Library Cataloguing-in-Publication Data
A catalogue record for this book is available from
the British Library.

ISBN: 978-1-78240-452-1

This book was conceived, designed and produced by
Ivy Press
58 West Street, Brighton BN1 2RA, UK

PUBLISHER Susan Kelly
CREATIVE DIRECTOR Michael Whitehead
EDITORIAL DIRECTOR Tom Kitch
ART DIRECTOR James Lawrence
COMMISSIONING EDITOR Stephanie Evans
PROJECT EDITOR Jamie Pumfrey
DESIGNER Susan McIntyre
ILLUSTRATOR Jamie Bush
ASSISTANT EDITOR Jenny Campbell

Printed in China

10 9 8 7 6 5 4 3 2

Contents

WELCOME

Founded on conquest, expanded by enterprise and ruled by compromise, London feels very different to other capital cities. Geographical convenience, exploited first by the Romans and then by the Anglo-Saxons, gave it two distinct centres. Settlement began in the east, at the first high point along the banks of the river Thames, and trade has remained there; the City of London or Square Mile, now simply one of the wider city's many administrative districts, is also one of the world's most important financial markets. Across town, well away from the sights, sounds and smells of commerce, the monarch, church and Parliament established themselves in Westminster. This book concentrates on those two hubs, plus the once-derelict docks that became the basis for a third. No grand plan or dictator's vision has shaped London, yet generations wrought fundamental changes that led the way in urban planning. The Georgians' quiet residential squares pioneered a new mode of living, while the Victorian

TO LONDON

railways were laid both over and below the ground – the latter, known to all as the Tube, was the first such enterprise to be constructed anywhere. Today London is identified with internationally renowned places of learning and art, sport and ceremony, shopping and worship. They have been designed by architects of historical stature, including Wren, Hawksmoor and Lutyens, important figures in the British context such as Lasdun, Holden and Scott, and contemporary global superstars like Rogers, Libeskind and the late Zaha Hadid, while little-known gems take their own place in this rich mix. Discover them all in these pages.

Capital city

London would not exist without the Thames, crossed now a dozen times by bridges yet initially and for centuries only by the bridge that bears its city's name.

Looking for Clues

London's evolving architectural story has always paralleled social and political change. The Great Fire in 1666 ravaged her heart; rebuilding took a decade but as individual homes were reconstructed, grand houses built along the Thames and shining white stone churches thrust into the sky, a capacity for renewal and continued growth was evident. The spread of Georgian hospitals, public squares and private housing suggested this was unstoppable. The secular vied with the sacred in the early years of Victoria's reign, noble

Note

A change in a building's name is shown below the main entry heading.

Georgian elegance, Victorian vision
The Enlightenment and its rationality means the London of today is still defined by streets of uniform terraced houses as historic patrons were joined by a new class of builder – the speculator. The great public works of the Victorians transformed the city further.

From splendour to Modernity
Bold Edwardian buildings show the power and the glory of the British Empire at its height, but within a decade the stripped-down plainness of Modernism began to appear on the streets of the city. Never fully welcomed, it did produce many delights.

edifices laying the foundations for a truly global city that a world war barely interrupted. In its aftermath modernity met with resistance yet popular culture embraced its new ways. Another shocking war introduced directed redevelopment, something London has seldom appreciated, and today private wealth is in the ascendant once more. Of course, the very best way to experience and understand all of these moments and more is by walking London's streets with this indispensable guide in your hand.

Post-war promise

As London was rebuilt, her architecture was dominated by Brutalism and Corporate Modernism, bare concrete and glass curtain walling coming to define the landscape. New places emerged for living and learning, working and playing, and the tower loomed above all.

Contemporary challenges

As Modernism finally dissipated, High Tech presaged the computing revolution, Postmodernism amusingly undermined Classicism and Deconstructivism took everything apart. London's architecture gained from the millennium and the Olympics but concerns over environmental awareness, scale and funding now dominate those of style.

Introduction

The capital was at first confined to the City, centred on the original London Bridge. This area was devastated by the Great Fire of 1666, and so our story begins with the outliers and scattered survivors as well as the fruits of the reconstruction that followed.

The architecture is predominantly Classical, using the forms and motifs of ancient Greece and Rome, or in the newer, more florid styles of the Renaissance and the Baroque. Strange and exotic, these imports were often toned down for domestic tastes.

Elegant elevations
Sir Christopher Wren's austere but attractive façades for the Royal Hospital Chelsea are Classically inspired.

Westminster Abbey

Location *20 Dean's Yard
London SW1*
Date *1246–1745*
Architects *unknown/
various architects*

Growing from a Benedictine monastery enlarged by Edward the Confessor into today's national home of ceremony and remembrance, Westminster – the name is literal, meaning the western counterpart to St Paul's – has a particularly royal history. It has no parish of its own, sits outside the control of bishops and has witnessed the coronation of every crowned English (and, later, British) monarch since 1066. It remains one of the greatest English Gothic constructions despite much alteration and refacing, while also borrowing heavily from the latest French thinking.

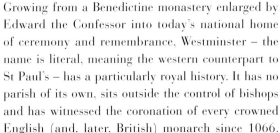

Perpendicular progress
Initially spread over three broad phases between the 13th and early 16th centuries, stylistic changes were surprisingly few until the late 1300s and the 'rational' verticals and horizontals of Perpendicular on the west front. Nicholas Hawksmoor's much later towers follow this in turn.

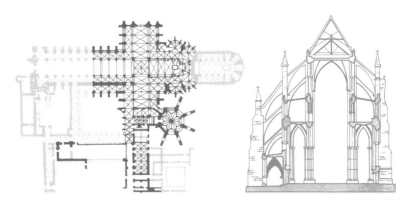

Plan

Henry III's replacement for the Norman original began with the French Gothic-influenced polygonal eastern apse and radiating chapels, although the long, three-bay transepts are English. A hiatus of a century divides the first four bays of the nave from the remainder.

Soaring section

French, too, is the extreme height – rising taller than any other English church, and from a very narrow base – and the flying buttresses needed for bracing. The gallery or triforium to the east may have housed spectator seating or been intended for additional chapels.

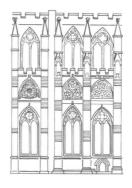

Subtle seams

Small changes, chiefly in the foils or lobes of the stone tracery, mark the different building periods of the nave, starting (left) with the east bay of the northern façade. Mere nuances separate the fourth bay, where work stopped in 1272, and the fifth.

Lady chapel

The half-medieval, half-Gothic church climaxes in Henry VII's tribute to his Tudor lineage. Respectfully attached to the far east end in 1510, its spectacular fan vaulting is unequalled. The precariously 'hanging' pendants are in fact the extended wedge stones of the structural roof arches.

229 & 230 Strand

Location *London WC2*
Date *1625 onwards*
Architect *unknown*

After the Romans left, Anglo-Saxon *Lundenwic*'s developing royal and ecclesiastical enclave in the west was linked to the established commercial centre in the east by a road hugging the foreshore of the Thames. Its current name reflects this – Strand is the German word for beach. Houses were erected along the new thoroughfare, the vast majority on plots that were deep but narrow because a street frontage was expensive. That pattern has largely endured despite repeated redevelopment. These houses are altered but very rare examples of those original structures.

Rare survivors
Probably the oldest remaining secular buildings in central London, No. 229, at least, escaped the Great Fire while No. 230 may have been home to the gatekeeper of Temple Bar, the western entry to the City formerly spanning the Strand at this point.

Space invader

The distinctive projection of the upper floors – seen here in more complete form elsewhere – is called jettying. A common way of maximising space, this had an unfortunate side effect – it helped spread the Great Fire as flames jumped easily from house to house.

Jetty joints

The timber frame of such houses needed complex connections. The curved piece is called coving and joints were pegged, not nailed. On the Strand properties the wood is plastered, giving protection from the weather and, to a degree, fire.

Bay window

Pushing the windows out from the façade is another way to gain more space, though these also scoop more light into the room. Almost as important are the improved views up and down the street, for amusement, convenience and security.

Stained glass

For almost 100 years the buildings were occupied by the Wig and Pen Club, whose membership was drawn from the journalists and lawyers working at the High Court opposite. Its commemorative window design was retained by the restaurant now on the site.

Covent Garden Piazza

Location *King Street London WC2*

Date *1629–37*

Architect *Inigo Jones*

Planning pioneer

Initially belonging to the Abbey (or Convent) of Westminster, the land was acquired by Henry VIII and subsequently granted to John Russell, the 1st Earl of Bedford. Francis, the 4th Earl, laid out the piazza, though Jones was appointed by Charles I.

The loss of all its earliest houses, insertion of the 19th-century covered market and general bustle of this popular venue disguise its beginnings as a groundbreaking piece of civic design by one of Britain's greatest Classical architects. New streets led to a large open space, edged with refined townhouses raised above arcaded walkways. An elegant church formed the focal point. Copied many times in the following century, Jones's concept would become one of London's defining features – the residential square.

Handsome barn

Bedford desired St Paul's Church to be 'not much better than a barn'; Jones promised him 'the handsomest barn in England'. Flanking screen walls and pavilion-like corner houses integrate the church with the piazza. Tuscan columns and a double square plan signal antique sources.

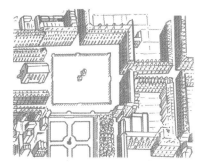

Urban order

Though ultimately deriving from ancient Roman precedents, Jones's scheme was informed by two recent developments: the Piazza d'Arme in Livorno and the Place des Vosges in Paris. The earl funded the streets, cellars and drains, but individual lessees bore the risk of building the houses speculatively.

Reversed entrance (below)

Probably in deference to Jones's wider plan, the church initially had its altar placed to the west. This was changed during construction so that liturgical and geographic east align and the west front now marks the way in.

Arcades

These represented a pragmatic quid pro quo – the public gained shelter, while the building tenant gained floor space above them. This public application of an idea that had been used in private religious architecture for some time began in Renaissance Italy.

Kew Palace

Location *Richmond Surrey*

Date *1631*

Architect *unknown*

Royal residence

Fortrey's house was later home to George II's eldest daughters. As part of a larger complex favoured by the royals and developed over time it was visited by George's descendants, including George III, and saw the death of Queen Charlotte.

The building now known as Kew Palace is one of several large private houses built along the Thames to the west of the capital in what was then countryside. Commissioned by Flemish merchant Samuel Fortrey, who had fled persecution on the Continent, it employs Classical styling but with subtle adaptations to honour Fortrey's heritage. The villa was nicknamed the Dutch House as a result. Such wilful but controlled rule-breaking came to be referred to as Mannerism.

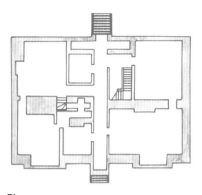

Plan

The basic layout can still be seen in the central corridor with a pair of rooms on either side, a configuration repeated on the upper floors. Both main façades – which are nearly identical – are seven bays wide, the outer ones broken (pushed) forward.

Beautiful brick

Laid – appropriately, but unusually for the time – in Flemish bond, where 'headers' and 'stretchers' alternate in the same course, the humble brick could be shaped by moulding (using a special wooden frame for the clay), cutting or rubbing (sanding after firing).

Dutch gables

These are the most obvious of the 'Netherlandish' elements. Double-curved, they are topped with triangular or segmental (rounded) pediments, a Classical device. Similarly Classical are the columns and rustication around the windows, all of which are skilfully done in brick.

Original decor

The interiors of the house have been reworked many times, but 17th-century plasterwork can still be seen decorating the ceiling of the Queen's Boudoir. The geometry of the ribbing is typical of the Renaissance, and the medallions contain reliefs depicting the five senses.

St Paul's Cathedral

Location
*St Paul's Churchyard
London EC4*
Date *1669–1711*
Architect *Christopher
Wren*

Appropriately perched on a hill at the highest point in the City of London, the new apostolic cathedral church of St Paul crowned Wren's career. He had already laid plans to remodel its dilapidated medieval predecessor when the Great Fire destroyed it. After doggedly promoting half a dozen successive variations over nine years, Wren finally received permission to rebuild to his own design, though even during construction he made changes. It is fitting that Wren lived to see it completed.

Layers and meanings
As built, Wren's stone colossus blends a wealth of influences including French Classicism, Italian Baroque and English Gothic. The latter generated the high nave and low aisles, but Wren raised the external walls to disguise this, unifying the structure and visually anchoring the dome.

Plan

Wren mixed the best in cathedral planning from both English medieval and international sources. The projecting towers resemble those at Wells, while a dome spanning both nave and aisles evokes Ely. The semicircular transept porches, however, may have an Italian precedent.

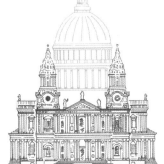

Double dome

Sitting on an attic above a peristyle or circular colonnade and finally a plain drum, the dome whose leaded ribbing matches those columns is not the same dome whose painted ceiling amazes inside; there are two, built either side of a structural brick cone.

West front

The lower level encompasses the aisles but the upper is only as wide as the nave, subtly undermining the sham walls. Paired pilasters, actually part of the intricate tower design, artfully fill the gap. St Paul himself features in statue and relief forms.

Vaulting ambition

Saucer domes, taken from Mansart's Val-de-Grâce, Paris and the Hagia Sophia, Constantinople, roof nave and aisles. Their fluid interplay with pilasters and columns peaks at the crossing, where double arches in the diagonal corners provide even more support for the main dome.

St Stephen Walbrook

Location *Walbrook London EC4*

Date *1672–80*

Architect *Christopher Wren*

Nondescript from the outside and even today quite hemmed in by other buildings, this retiring church by Wren has spatial qualities that become apparent only on the inside. As an 'auditory church' it epitomised the Church of England's new thinking after the Restoration, whereby no part of the ceremony was to be hidden from the congregation who could therefore hear (and often now see) everything, yet also seemingly features England's first Renaissance dome. The steeple came later, possibly from Wren's pupil Nicholas Hawksmoor.

Wren gem

Regarded as one of his best works, St Stephen was personally designed by Wren – it was his parish church, and the only Great Fire rebuild to begin construction in 1672. Aspects anticipate his achievement at St Paul's, building of which started later.

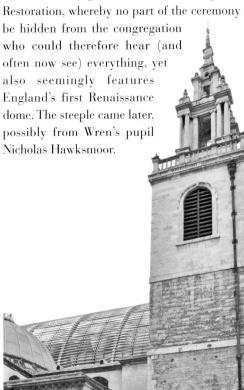

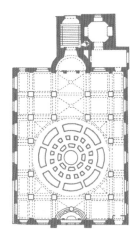

Plan

A combined ground floor and reflected ceiling plan clearly shows how Wren effortlessly merged a traditional English longitudinal (cross) layout, complete with short but discernibly separate nave, chancel and transepts, and a continental composition centred on a dome.

Entrance detail

Above the main door sits an attractive oval window surmounted by a convincingly naturalistic carved garland. Most other decoration is found where it would have been seen, on the east and north façades; this last faced a market place originally.

Perfect plaster

Fine Classical plasterwork includes the horizontal entablature above the Corinthian columns, the undersides of the arches and especially the recessed panels or coffers of the dome itself. This would find its counterpart in stone at St Paul's.

Squaring the circle

Further ingenuity resolved Wren's wish for the dome to stand on columns that faithfully followed the right angles of the longitudinal plan. Three columns per corner generate arches, which in turn reach the dome; small spandrel panels fill the gaps.

Royal Hospital Chelsea

Location *Royal Hospital Road, London SW3*
Date *1681–92*
Architect *Christopher Wren*

Graceful retirement

Wren's campus gave dignity and amenity to those who had served their country. Its simple but appealing proportions and materials, the latter largely red brick with stone quoins or corner pieces, anticipated the terraced housing of the forthcoming Georgian era.

Directly inspired by Louis XIV's Invalides in Paris, begun in 1676, London's own permanent charitable home for army veterans – or 'land soldiers', as Charles II's royal warrant described them – was laid out by Wren to a generous plan on a rural, riverside site. A central range housed the communal facilities, with two 'long wards' extending forward to accommodate the residents themselves. Four further wings, perpendicular to these, created three courtyards altogether. Today, the red-jacketed Chelsea Pensioners are famous worldwide.

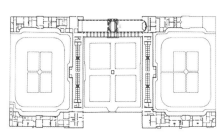

Plan

By careful placement of doorways, passages and stairs, Wren maintained the sense of camaraderie that is a fundamental part of being a soldier while granting each man privacy and independence. Four smaller pavilions to the east and the west housed additional residents.

Figure court

The elevations, Doric portico and colonnade (complete with Latin inscription by Wren) form a harmonious whole. The Great Hall and chapel are lit by double-height windows; the considerable expanse of plain brickwork is subtly relieved by recessed panels above and below.

Living wings

More than 475 men were settled mainly in four-storey wings that contained, on each floor, 1.8 m (6 ft)-square 'berths' for one man placed back-to-back along a central wall. The end blocks were houses for the hospital's governors, each of which filled all four levels of its wing.

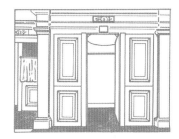

Personal space

Though enlarged several times and modernised, the essence of Wren's berths survives. Formed from wooden partitions and decorated with Classical pilasters (flat columns) and mouldings, the upper panels open like shutters to give views onto the communal corridor.

Royal Hospital for Seamen

Location *King William Walk, London SE10*

Date *1696–1751*

Architects *Christopher Wren, Nicholas Hawksmoor, John James, John Vanbrugh, Thomas Ripley*

Overcoming inauspicious beginnings, including adaptation of an unfinished new palace and physical division of the planned single building into two halves to avoid blocking Queen Mary II's view, the sailors' equivalent of the Chelsea hospital, at Greenwich, is one of the most magnificent and important architectural compositions in the country. Wren responded confidently to the brief, with other architects later working within his overall scheme. After 1873 the hospital was used as the Royal Naval College for 125 years.

Coming style
The influence of the Baroque, a mode of grandeur and incident from continental Europe, was somewhat weakened by the distance it had to travel to England; Wren outlined his southern buildings with many dozen Classical, Doric columns rather than manipulate its walls.

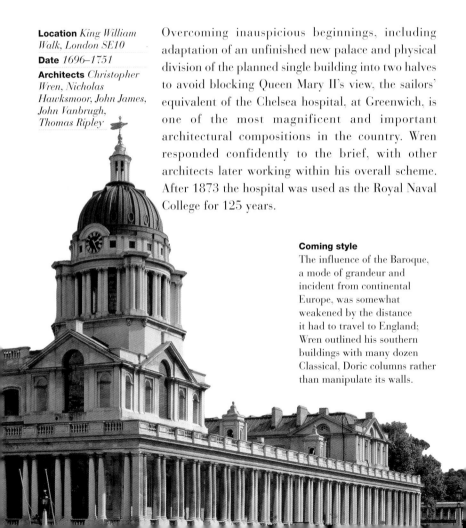

Façade

Two identical long elevations, together with a shorter pair to another design, form the quadrangle of King Charles's Building. One of two riverside wings, it incorporates the only retained part of the abandoned palace. Wren fuses Classical details with Baroque swagger.

Powerful prospect (below)

An aerial view shows how adeptly Wren was able to accommodate the royal command to split the building: the exquisite framing of the pre-existing Queen's House that results appears premeditated. Domes cap the Painted Hall and the chapel, consecrated several decades later.

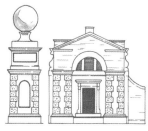

Classic portal

Wren united Classical motifs just as effectively at a smaller scale, here the West Gate's piers and porter's lodge. The finial is a terrestrial globe marked with lines of latitude and longitude, and sits above a relief carving of anchors, sails, blocks and tackle.

Painted Hall

Allegorical imagery executed by and under the supervision of James Thornhill covers the double-height space intended as a refectory but soon found to be too small for the purpose. The king and queen triumph over Tyranny, amidst the Seasons, the Elements, Trade and more.

Kensington Palace

Location *Kensington Gardens, London W8*

Date *1689–1727*

Architects *Christopher Wren, Nicholas Hawksmoor, William Benson*

Keen to improve the king's health, William III and Mary II bought a Jacobean mansion in what was then a village, commissioning a busy Wren to turn it into a suitable royal residence. He added blocks to each corner of the old house and two wings closed by an archway topped with a clock tower to the west, making a new entrance. The palace was the last outside central London to be lived in by a reigning monarch.

Royal connections

Residents have included Diana, Princess of Wales and the Duke and Duchess of Cambridge (William and Kate). William III laid a private, gas-lit road to link his new palace with its predecessor, St James's. It survives as Rotten Row, a riding track.

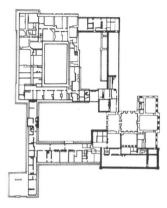

Plan

Wren's initial expansions appear at lower right, with Hawksmoor's King's Gallery forming a new south front. Clock Court is the large space in the centre. Queen Mary's Wren apartments and her own later gallery and staff wing sit top right.

Clock Court

The French influence prevailing at the time is shown in Wren's formation of a fully enclosed courtyard or *cour d'honneur* to the west. This also gave privacy to the royal apartments, which were now on the far side of the house.

Cupola Room

George I hired a young William Kent to decorate Benson's insertion between two of Wren's corner wings. Kent, trained as a painter, later moved into architecture and his concept of total design seduced society. A new phase in taste and Britain's monarchy had begun.

South front

Hawksmoor's façade continues the spirit of Wren's work, with understated form and detail in service of a wider harmony. So widespread and consistent was this kind of architecture that it is often identified as 'William and Mary', after its prolific patrons.

Houses, Queen Anne's Gate

Location *Queen Anne's Gate, London SW1*
Date *1704–05*
Architect *unknown*

This small street, sandwiched between busy Petty France to the south and the open spaces of St James's Park to the north and dominated by a bulky 1970s office block, contains terraces of houses from the first and last quarters of the 18th century. Many have been altered but amongst the former are some of the best-preserved in the capital. Developed speculatively, they differed in size and level of decoration but all had wainscoting, or timber panelling, along the lower walls and marble or Portland stone fireplaces.

Last of their kind
Three groups of houses date from this period: Nos. 15–25, 26–32 and 40–46. The western end of the street was originally a square, separated from the eastern end by a low, railed wall. This accounts for the L-shaped No. 15, which turned the square's south-east corner.

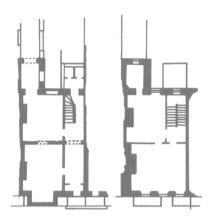

Typical plan

The smaller houses, like Nos. 44–46, have a simple layout but it is as efficient and logical as those of the larger examples. The plan also drives the exterior appearance of both, as seen in their characteristically regular fenestration.

Even elevation

As seen at No. 30, geometrically derived rhythm gives a pleasing look to the Georgian terrace. Sliding sash windows minimise disturbance to this aesthetic when opened for ventilation, unlike casements. Stone banding delineates the principal floors, with their taller windows.

Surviving stair

The oak main stair of No. 26 is original. Delightful spiral balusters group together to form newels. The landing has a deeply carved frieze running around it at first-floor level; such stairs often only served this storey, as upper floors were used by servants.

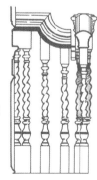

Door hood

The wooden canopy or door hood of No. 17 is elaborately carved with foliage, flowers and a face. Acorns terminate the three pendants. In later Georgian housing all decoration, even the window keystones (modelled as heads on these houses), would be pared away.

St Mary le Strand

Location *Strand London WC2*

Date *1714–17*

Architect *James Gibbs*

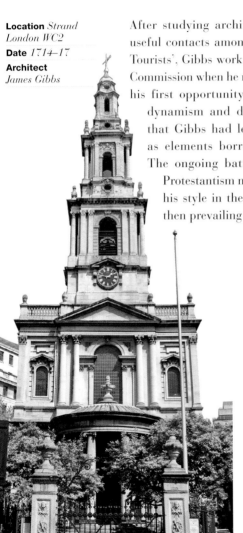

After studying architecture in Rome and making useful contacts amongst influential English 'Grand Tourists', Gibbs worked for the 1710 New Churches Commission when he returned to Britain. This yielded his first opportunity to build, demonstrating the dynamism and drama of the Italian Baroque that Gibbs had learned on his travels, as well as elements borrowed from Wren's St Paul's. The ongoing battle between Catholicism and Protestantism meant Gibbs soon had to modify his style in the face of the calmer Classicism then prevailing in England.

Island life

Though designed 'in the round', St Mary was originally closer to buildings to the north and faced the end of a terrace of houses to the east, across a street. The widening of the Strand and the formation of Aldwych left it more isolated from 1900.

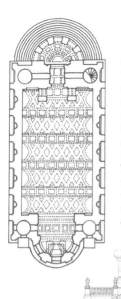

Plan

The narrow entrance to the west suddenly expands into what is one single space, as Gibbs dispensed with aisles to increase the impact of the interior. The depth of the walls' articulation, with pilasters behind niches behind columns, is clear.

Apse

The east end reflects the west in plan and elevation but the column orders are now Composite over Corinthian, a more intense experience. A slice of barrel vaulting neatly joins the apse to the nave, just one of Gibbs's adroitly handled geometric intersections.

West front

Semicircular steps and a porch centre the entrance. Its façade initiates the energetic pattern of triangular pediments above segmental and Corinthian columns over Ionic that wraps around the remainder of the exterior. Such animation was especially appropriate for a building passed on all sides.

Coffered ceiling

Spandrels shaped into diamonds and triangles alternating with squares form the ceiling; delicate, fern-like fronds fill their centres and decorate the ribs. The density and intricacy of this arrangement prefigures the work of Robert Adam later in the century.

Christ Church, Spitalfields

Location
*Commercial Street
London E1*

Date *1714–29*

Architect *Nicholas
Hawksmoor*

The East End was especially important for the New Churches Commission following an influx of French Huguenot weavers and Nonconformists to the area. Hawksmoor was its surveyor throughout the entire commission period, and undertook site inspection, land purchase and what would now be known as community liaison. Wren was a commissioner. It was thus no real surprise when the man who had been Wren's architectural disciple was finally given a chance to practise his own style with this and several other churches.

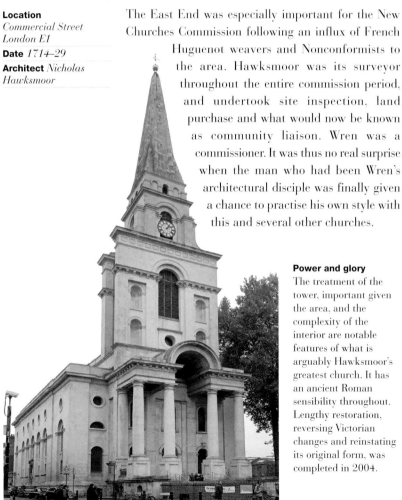

Power and glory

The treatment of the tower, important given the area, and the complexity of the interior are notable features of what is arguably Hawksmoor's greatest church. It has an ancient Roman sensibility throughout. Lengthy restoration, reversing Victorian changes and reinstating its original form, was completed in 2004.

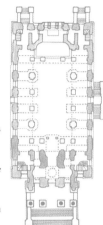

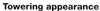

Plan

The large western portico and tower base lead to two colonnades marking the side aisles. Additional doors to the north (now lost) and south would have made a cross-axis – the differing columns are symmetrical around the remaining southern entrance, too.

Towering appearance

The immense steeple more than fulfils the exhortation to signal the church's presence. Its lower part adapts the motif of the hooded, tripartite Venetian window but doubles its height; the equally imposing portico models this in three dimensions and exactly matches the tower's width.

Interior

High bases for the Composite columns allowed for box pews. Aisles are roofed between each pair of columns with individual transverse barrel vaults bearing polygonal coffering, accentuating the cross-axis. This recalls the ancient Basilica of Maxentius in Rome.

Planes of stone

Toward the north and south, the exterior walls are startlingly modern – almost Moderne – in their plainness. Two windows in each bay are framed by a single double-height arch and are unornamented, save some details. Hawksmoor aimed to awe onlookers.

Location Map

With the beginnings of London's chief sources of power – trade, the monarchy and the church – buildings cluster accordingly, whether in the east, where the Romans matter-of-factly bridged the Thames at the first suitable spot they encountered, or the quieter, more rustic land to the west. What is now the West End developed naturally between the two. The aristocracy pervaded all three.

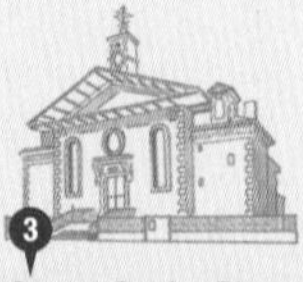

③ Covent Garden Piazza
King Street, WC2
page 16

④ Kew Palace
Richmond, Surrey
page 18

⑤ St Paul's Cathedral
St Paul's Churchyard, EC4 *page 20*

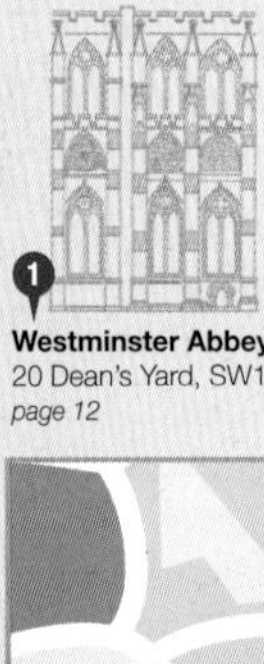

① Westminster Abbey
20 Dean's Yard, SW1
page 12

② 229 & 230 Strand
WC2 *page 14*

Richmond

④

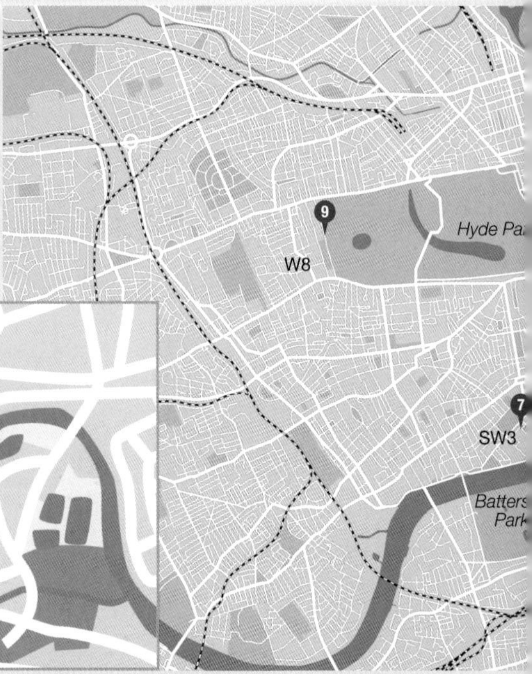

⑨

W8

Hyde Pa..

⑦

SW3

Batters.. Park

6
St Stephen Walbrook
Walbrook, EC4
page 22

7
Royal Hospital Chelsea
Royal Hospital Road,
SW3 *page 24*

8
Royal Hospital for Seamen
King William Walk,
SE10 *page 26*

9
Kensington Palace
Kensington Gardens,
W8 *page 28*

10
Houses, Queen Anne's Gate
Queen Anne's Gate,
SW1 *page 30*

11
St Mary le Strand
Strand, WC2
page 32

12
Christ Church, Spitalfields
Commercial Street, E1
page 34

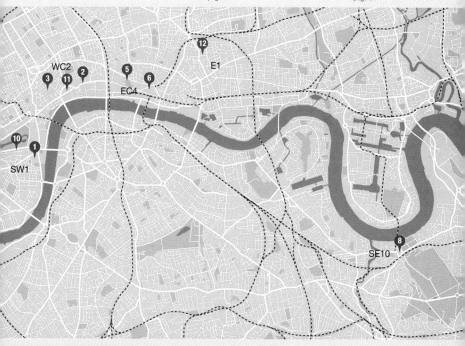

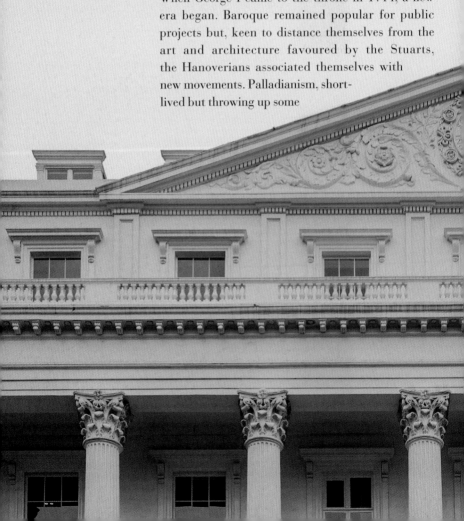

Introduction

When George I came to the throne in 1714, a new era began. Baroque remained popular for public projects but, keen to distance themselves from the art and architecture favoured by the Stuarts, the Hanoverians associated themselves with new movements. Palladianism, short-lived but throwing up some of the greatest houses in Britain let alone London, and the more rigorous Greek Revival saw Classical principles applied more originally and systematically. Secular institutions and civic order predominated but also, and arguably above all else, the mass housing that is so identified with the period.

Graceful expanses
The refined Neoclassical styling, delicate decoration and repetitive motifs of John Nash's Carlton House Terrace typify Georgian style.

St George, Bloomsbury

Location
*Bloomsbury Way
London WC1*

Date *1716–31*

Architect *Nicholas
Hawksmoor*

Of all the churches Hawksmoor built for the New Churches Commission, St George was the last, perhaps the most intriguing and certainly the most compromised by later alterations. As surveyor he was required to find only sites compatible with the east-west alignment of traditional English churches, yet here he acquired a narrow, defiantly north-south plot. The manner in which Hawksmoor reconciled this conflict confirms his ability as a manipulator of space, while the dramatic exterior is characteristic of his highly individualistic approach. Both are legible again following restoration.

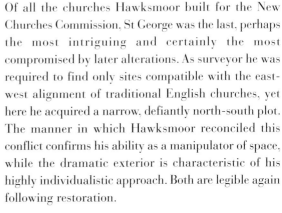

Church warden
Located in one of London's most intractable slums – its spire, complete with statue of George I dressed as a Roman emperor, is visible in the background of Hogarth's campaigning print *Gin Lane*, published 20 years later – St George was a beacon for Christianity's succour.

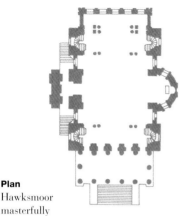

Plan

Hawksmoor masterfully disposed altar (in an eastern apse), tower (opposite, flanked by entrance stairs) and portico (to the south, and only for show) to create the desired alignment. The square defined by the four pairs of columns further disguises the actual orientation.

Vivid volume

The nave is a cube lit by clerestory windows in its upper level. Northern and southern galleries, originally seating for the local dukes but also helping maintain the congregation's focus on the eastern altar when entering from the west, have been reconstructed.

Urban signposts

The site was also tightly enclosed by houses, an additional challenge. Placing the unique steeple to one side allowed its entire height to be read immediately, acting as a powerful marker. The six-columned Corinthian portico on the confined southern frontage reinforced the church's authority.

Beasts of Britain

The striking pyramidal spire is based on the Tomb of Mausolus at Halicarnassus. More relevant are the startling, vigorous sculptures of lions and unicorns, symbols of England and Scotland since the accession of James VI of Scotland and I of England now validated by the 1707 Acts of Union.

St Martin-in-the-Fields

Location
Trafalgar Square
London WC2
Date *1721–26*
Architect *James Gibbs*

Erected as a result of a parish petition to the monarch following concerns over the deteriorated state of the existing church, the new St Martin-in-the-Fields became a touchstone for architects and a landmark for central London even before the laying out 100 years later of Trafalgar Square, to which it now forms the north-eastern gateway. Wren was an inspiration, but the Baroque also practised by Gibbs – already tempered – was soon further tamed by Palladianism.

Export licence

With the Royal Arms of George I filling the portico's tympanum, an absence of figurative sculpture and the use of plain window glass, this was a thoroughly Anglican church. Copies were soon seen throughout Britain's colonies, especially America, encouraged by Gibbs publishing a book of his designs.

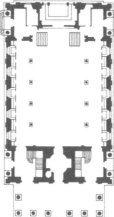

Plan

Gibbs placed his steeple directly over the centre of the west front, yet this integration was felt by some to be undermined by the large portico. The aisled nave narrows at the east to form the chancel, just one homage to Wren.

Interior

The Corinthian columns continue inside, supporting an elliptical or flat principal ceiling and saucer domes over the aisles on square blocks of entablature above each capital. Lavish plasterwork on a heavenly theme ties both together for an extremely elegant whole.

Variable geometry

The tiered steeple employs different shapes to distinguish it. The lowest stage, housing the bells, is square in plan, the lantern above is octagonal and the spire appears circular due to its taper. Urns, columns and oculi make their own contribution.

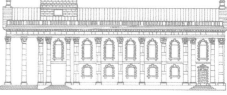

Monumental massing

A single, giant Corinthian order is carried around the entire body of the church, as columns at each end and immediately beneath the spire, and as pilasters elsewhere. The treatment of the window surrounds – blocked, like square beads on a string – is a Gibbs favourite.

Old Admiralty
Ripley Building

Civic order

As the Navy expanded, so did its buildings; upcoming architect Robert Adam's courtyard screen was added in 1761, Admiralty House to the south in 1788 and the massive western extension, with its distinctive towers, in 1905. Ripley's block lost its residential function in 1868.

Somewhat hidden by augmentations and extensions, what is effectively Britain's earliest office block survives relatively unchanged. Built for the Board of Admiralty – the men who had operational control over the Royal Navy – as individual apartments along with shared meeting and other rooms, Ripley's building reflected the emergence of dedicated provision for the organs of state in a new age of imperial power. Architecturally its quiet solemnity contrasts with the late Victorian and Edwardian hulks that surround it.

Location *Whitehall London SW1*
Date *1723–26*
Architect *Thomas Ripley*

Men-of-war

This ground-floor plan of 1794 shows how the building was divided into separate residences for each Lord Commissioner of the Admiralty. The wings' internal divisions do not match those of the façades, which are split into groups of three bays.

Plain portico

Before Adam's screen partly obscured the view, the giant-order Ionic portico was more dominant. It is higher than Classical theory stipulates in order to bring more light into the top floor. The tympanum of its triangular pediment displays a carved ship's anchor.

Courtyard plan

The simple arrangement of wings projecting from a centre block was copied from the previous Admiralty building. Stone quoins, cornice and string courses aside, the brick building is rigorously utilitarian, having more in common with military barracks. This would change.

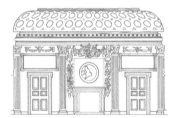

Board room

Ripley's space is lined with oak panelling, Corinthian pilasters, beautiful pearwood carvings of garlands, trophies and navigation instruments by the great Grinling Gibbons and a large wind compass, all taken from the earlier building. The coffered, coved ceiling belongs with subsequent work.

St John, Smith Square

Location
*30 Smith Square
London SW1*

Date *1713–28*

Architect *Thomas Archer*

The Church of St John the Evangelist has not fulfilled that role for over 70 years after burning in the Blitz. Its situation in the quiet backstreets of Westminster was well suited to post-war life as a recital hall, but it was the most expensive and one of the more arresting of the 50 new places of worship called for by the New Churches Commission. Confidently Baroque with links to the work of Francesco Borromini, Classicism appears only restrainedly.

Bold Baroque

Several elements combine to make one of the strongest statements of the Baroque in London, including the convex quadrants between each arm, variation in articulation and the widely broken pediments, each with its own small broken pediment within.

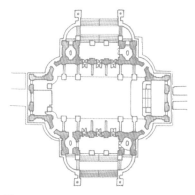

Plan

Seemingly a Greek cross (one with arms of equal length) from the outside, principally due to the twin staircases, the church has in fact a pronounced east-west bias. Entrance loggias buffering the nave and four pairs of internal columns emphasise this.

Ambiguous space

By the subtle use of vaulting, columns and their entablature, the eye can be led along both axes within the body of the church with equal ease. The space can thus be comprehended centrally or longitudinally, simultaneously according with continental and English practice.

Square deal

Originally far more exposed, St John is today tightly yet comfortably enclosed, near-uniform red brick a foil to its Portland stone and each façade aligned with a street. It is an extremely rare example of a building being enhanced by later developments.

Queen Anne's footstool

The towers create a highly animated skyline. This, their curving complexity and the innovation of the columns' circular entablature and bases are characteristic of the Baroque, these last showing Archer modifying Classicism. One legend blames the controversial towers on Queen Anne's order that the church should look like her upturned footstool.

Chiswick House

Location
*Burlington Lane
London W4*

Date *1726–29*

Architect *Lord
Burlington (Richard
Boyle, 3rd Earl of
Burlington)*

The 17th-century Italian architect Andrea Palladio popularised ancient Roman architecture through his gem-like country villas. His work was rediscovered by a small group of cultured English gentlemen through a translation of his *Four Books of Architecture*. Burlington, helped by William Kent, championed these ideals with his own Chiswick House. Best understood as a place for summer entertaining – it had no kitchen and no heating in the principal rooms – it was also a statement of intent for the new English architectural movement Burlington had started: Palladianism.

Splendid isolation

Linked by a wing to Burlington's Jacobean mansion until it was demolished, the villa's Palladian precision extended to the layout of the gardens and the design and even placement of urns, statues, mirrors and furniture, much of which was architectural in character.

Plan

The careful disposition of differently shaped rooms about a central hall is a quintessentially Palladian concept. Burlington welcomed visitors on the first floor in the double-height Tribunal or Saloon, with its Roman coffered dome, before taking them through the interlinked spaces.

Triple Gallery

A circle, a rectangle and an octagon together make up the Gallery. It had some paintings but primarily displayed itself – that is, an exquisitely integrated series of volumes, doorways, windows and arched passages. Classical niches, panelling and architectural ornament added further interest.

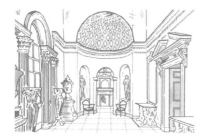

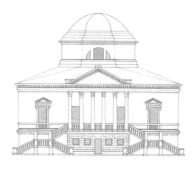

Perfect symmetry

The clarity of design is largely taken from a villa in Vincenza by a pupil of Palladio. The best rooms are on the first floor or *piano nobile*, above the dirt and where the air was fresher. Inigo Jones, another Palladio devotee, was also an influence.

Study in blue

Burlington's study, finished in sumptuous blue velvet, was also a shrine to Palladio, with many of his drawings on show, and Jones – his portrait appeared over a pedimented door. The paired ceiling brackets are a 16th-century Italian device.

Mansion House

Working from home

The building is much altered inside, but its exterior – complete with side elevations busier than purists like Burlington would have preferred – remains largely intact. Railings, a small forecourt and the dog-leg flights of the entrance stairs all fell victim to road widening.

This prestigious new home for the Lord Mayor of London was a statement in the new Palladian style. The need to fit apartments, a courtroom, service areas and large entertainment spaces into a constricted City site led Dance to place the latter across the building and the necessary courtyard on the first floor, open to the sky like the atrium of a Roman house. Ideas for the interiors were borrowed from William Kent and Colen Campbell, another adherent of Palladianism. The Mayoralty is now a post of advocacy for the Square Mile.

Location *Walbrook, London EC4*
Date *1739–52; 1795*
Architects *George Dance the Elder; George Dance the Younger*

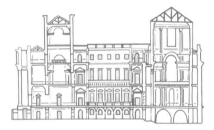

High ceremony

As built, the *piano nobile* was taken up by a procession of state rooms for guests, including the courtyard, and climaxed in the cavernous Egyptian Hall; the sequence continued on the second floor with the Ballroom and Hall balcony.

Enduring decoration

After 40 years the courtyard was roofed over by Dance's son for extra space but its plasterwork survives. This fine piece by George Fewkes alludes to the wealth of the seas. The unhampered form signals the late Baroque-era Rococo idiom.

Absent attics

Attic storeys contained the upper levels of the two great function rooms, retaining their impact while permitting them to be positioned higher in order to free space below. The attics were removed decades later, with lower ceilings installed to Neoclassical designs.

Ancient inspiration

The 'Egyptian Hall' actually had its genesis in Roman architect Vitruvius's understanding of ancient Greek public buildings, which Burlington had already interpreted in his York Assembly Rooms. Scale is everything, from the giant-order Corinthian columns and round-headed window to the sculpted panels above.

Spencer House

Location
*27 St James's Place
London SW1*

Date *1756–66; 1783*

Architects *John Vardy;
James Stuart;
Henry Holland*

Facing change

A layered façade with a rhythmic run of engaged Doric columns frames the *piano nobile*, atop a channelled lower floor. A rusticated terrace – made by building over part of the street – lifts the entire edifice above the garden and park beyond.

Almost all of London's grand 18th-century mansions have been lost, leaving that built for John, 1st Earl Spencer, as one of the last of its kind. Importantly, it is also one of the best – connecting Palladianism and the later Neoclassicism through what was essentially a single campaign by two architects. Vardy, a pupil of William Kent, completed the exterior, ground-floor and upper-floor layout before the more practised (and scholarly – as evidenced by his nickname, 'Athenian') Stuart replaced him. Holland modified both men's work after the earl's death.

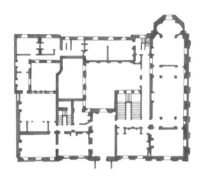

Plan

Spencer's house sits partly on a plot assembled by the previous lessee, for whom Vardy made firm designs but who died before construction began. Additional land acquired by Spencer drove an amended, larger version for himself; its projecting bow housed the Palm Room.

Total artwork

A design thought to be by Inigo Jones and a Roman temple frieze came together in this extraordinary space. Gilded plaster palm fronds wrap around half columns to symbolise fertility and the ancient Greek belief that all architecture derives from natural forms.

Sparer stairhall

Stuart's more attenuated Neoclassicism arrived quietly at the top of the main stair, where Vardy's Ionic pilasters received connecting garlands and an entablature with palmettes and an arched recess flanked by doorways echoed his Venetian window on the half-landing below.

Higher calling

Directly above Vardy's Dining Room sits the Great Room. Here Stuart once again uses Roman and Greek sources, particularly for the coffered ceiling. Its deep coving also prefigures the work of Adam, whose house interiors unified floor, walls and ceiling in a single decorative scheme.

Somerset House

Location *Strand London WC2*

Date *1775–1801*

Architect *William Chambers*

Quiet quad

Behind the narrow street frontage, which was reserved for the institutions given its cachet and convenience, the campus expands dramatically. Offices are set around a large courtyard, each wing resembling a separate palazzo. The effect is that of a town square.

This building for learned societies and government bureaucracy replaced the riverside home of Edward 'Protector' Seymour, 1st Duke of Somerset. Steeped in Classical theory and thoroughly grounded in current practice both in England and elsewhere, Chambers sought to establish a definitive set of principles for Palladian architecture, albeit applying them here with touches of individuality such as altering the generally accepted hierarchy of the orders. Occupancies eventually changed, while Joseph Bazalgette's stupendous Embankment decisively divorced Somerset House from its watery context in the late 19th century.

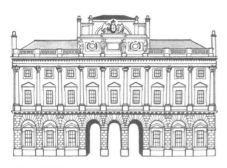

Strand side

Chambers replicated the old ducal home's gracious Classical Strand façade almost exactly, believing (wrongly) that Jones had designed it. Two new buildings he had encountered abroad – the Palazzo Poli behind the Trevi Fountain in Rome and the Paris Mint – were also influential.

Marine mask

Eight keystones representing particular English rivers, carved by Joseph Wilton and Agostino Carlini, form part of an extensive programme of commemorative and symbolic sculpture. Its placement amidst the architecture is Roman but the subject matter is firmly British.

Entrance exam

Either side of the dynamically vaulted Doric vestibule were the societies, including the Royal Academy of Arts. The semicircular stair beyond the Doric column screen hints at a number of sinuous, intricately balustraded examples within the complex, chiefly that serving the Seaman's Hall.

River range

Four times longer than the north block, this held the administrative Navy Board. Below it, a heavily rusticated base once gave directly onto the Thames for barge access. Chambers embraced the sloping plot elsewhere, with deep light wells for extra storeys below courtyard level.

Bedford Square

Location *London WC2*
Date *1775–86*
Architects *unknown/ various architects*

A century and a half after Inigo Jones's prototype at Covent Garden, purely residential squares were commonplace and the now dukes of Bedford returned to the idea elsewhere on their estate. The terraces of houses, each deploying an Ionic-order, pedimented centrepiece to simulate a single villa, were set around a private garden, a valuable amenity even then as London grew. Primarily a convivial enclave for the rising middle classes, the square's town-planning function was nevertheless obvious. This is an outstanding example of both, preserved intact.

Cover storey
The handsome appearance of Georgian terraces often belies ruthlessly parsimonious construction cynically driven by the length of the initial lease. Exterior walls just half a brick thick, pre-cast 'sculpture' of Eleanor Coade's artificial stone and stucco for porticos and other architectural detail were common.

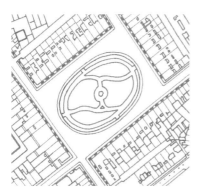

Plot

Bedford Square is not at all symmetrical, neither in its roads nor those centrepieces, which vary in width from three bays to seven. Behind the small backyards stood their respective mews, stables and coach houses, with servant accommodation above.

Skeleton service

The medieval plot shape persisting, the houses were two rooms deep but only one wide, plus a corridor with a staircase. Cost-conscious builders used excavated earth to raise the road level, meaning cellars only needed digging out to half their final depth, a useful economy.

Class distinction

Speculators now followed pattern books that simplified Classical principles and proportions. A memory of the originals thus survives in the rusticated doorcase surround, single taller *piano nobile* storey and entablature-like cornice. This systemic approach produced remarkable consistency across the capital.

Variation on a theme

A greater variety is found within such properties as each was fitted out by its builder to target different buyers, or the final purchaser himself. The delicate ceiling plasterwork of No. 47 is emblematic of Neoclassicism.

Bank of England

Location
*Threadneedle Street
London EC2*

Date *1732–34;
1765–88; 1788–1827;
and later, including
1923–39*

Architects *George
Sampson; Robert Taylor;
John Soane; and others,
including Herbert Baker*

Though initiated and today dominated by the work of others, the architecture of the nation's central bank is considered here because of the unifying, dramatic and highly original elements added at the turn of the 19th century by one of Britain's greatest practitioners. Soane's mighty, impenetrable perimeter wall was in contrast to his top-lit banking halls, their domes penetrated by ethereal light. Soane's wall remains but his domes endure only in imperfect reconstruction, following erasure and comprehensive rebuilding by Baker between the world wars.

Security screen

After extending the bank's footprint to the northern edge of its street block, Soane redid Taylor's southern walls to match his own and replaced Sampson's Threadneedle Street entrance. Inside the coursed wall, now freshly cleaned, Baker's blocks rise.

Payment plan

Soane advanced his predecessors' language of circles and domes, with their sources in antiquity, and conjured sophisticated axial rotations. The 'prow' or Tivoli Corner imitates the Roman Temple of Vesta, whose rosette capitals embellish the entire wall. Baker opened it as a pedestrian cut-through.

Customer window

Either side of the entrance Soane's meticulous rhythm of Corinthian articulation – now pilasters, now columns – is carried along the wall and around its corners. Blind openings, some now modified, provide additional depth. Soane's attic storey was supplanted by the balustrade seen today.

Attracting interest

The Museum inhabits a good 1980s reconstruction of Soane's Bank Stock Office, otherwise known only through haunting monochrome photographs. A shallow pendentive dome (one contiguous with its arched supports) confirms Soane as a master manipulator of space and light, the essence of architecture.

Manager meeting

Baker resited many columns, caryatids (pillars in human form) and fixtures from the previous phases of building, and also entire rooms. The Court Room is Taylor's, moved up to the first floor and with its Neoclassical decoration simplified.

The Nash Route

Location
*Carlton House Terrace
to Regent's Park
London SW1 to NW1*

Date *1812–34*

Architects *John Nash
(masterplan and some
buildings), various
architects*

Park Crescent
Ionic colonnades front
the built half of an
intended circus and
evoke Nash's own
Quadrant lower
down. Ahead lies the
enticement of Regent's
Park with its 'natural'
lake, a true expression
of the Roman notion of
rus in urbe or 'country
in town'.

Nash's commission from Frederick, the Prince Regent, to run a road from his palace of Carlton House in Piccadilly north across Oxford Street and Marylebone Road to a picturesque new park scattered with Italianate villas is one of the most important pieces of town planning in London's history. Though much of the architecture has been lost, isolated fragments and the elegant pattern it still traces through the city allow this *via triumphalis* – part royal whim on a grand scale, part pioneering metropolitan improvement – to be appreciated.

Reshaping a city

There were demolitions, but disruption (and costs) were minimised by following the existing Swallow Street below Oxford Circus and merging with the Adams' Portland Place above it. Skirting downmarket Soho also drew wealthier clients from the west while protecting royal dignity.

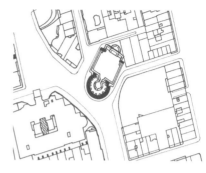

Turning points

Where the route changed direction Nash guided traffic smoothly into the next stretch. His All Souls, Langham Place church, its drum portico with circular spire acting as a pivot, remains; Regent Street's curved Quadrant was later rebuilt but to the same plan.

Cultured club

The Athenaeum stands on one side of Waterloo Place, the southernmost part of the route, balanced by the former United Services Club on the other. Decimus Burton's austere Greek Revival exterior, largely untouched, demonstrates the more academic tone of the period.

Moving houses

After the Prince Regent's accession as George IV he moved to Buckingham House; Nash planned two runs of Neoclassical houses to replace the unwanted palace. Their form is as composed as the rest – the raised terrace and basement precluded the need for visually intrusive mews.

Burlington Arcade

Location
Between Piccadilly and Burlington Gardens London W1

Date *1818–19*

Architect *Samuel Ware*

Inspired by Nash's just-completed Royal Opera Arcade nearby, the first true day-lit covered shopping street in Britain, Lord George Cavendish's Burlington Arcade is a much grander affair. Stretching for 180 m (almost 600 ft) and with shops on both sides rather than one, it was erected speculatively alongside his London home. Architecturally, the arcade pointed the way to a future of iron and glass; sociologically, the obsession of today with shopping – and shopping as theatre, where the customer appears almost as important as the seller – had begun

Shopping centre

Burlington's development popularised the pastime of strolling, browsing and buying in protected comfort. The concept spread throughout Europe, most notably to Brussels, Paris and Milan, and returned to Piccadilly with the Princes Arcade of 1930, the last to be built in London.

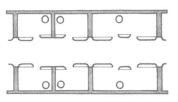

Making an entrance

Ware's arched portal featured clusters of three-quarter Ionic columns, the same order being repeated inside. This was lost in the Edwardian era, though the current upper-level arcading is a close copy. The wide street entrance is from 1931.

Architectural promenade

The generous skylights along the entire length of the arcade and the two-storey bay windows (a third level above the roof provided living quarters) mimicked a street but excluded its inconveniences. The shop-fronts varied in width, height and shape.

Boutique appeal

The regularity of the structural arches is answered within the bays they define by three types of shop units – single, double or heightened double – arranged in a different rhythm. This gave flexibility for tenants and avoided monotony for shoppers.

Window display

Selected units have their doors set on a slight diagonal, another original feature. This gave more prominence to the window display and subtle 'kerb' appeal. Larger sheets of plate glass replaced smaller panes within a few decades and some small shops were combined.

British Museum

Location
*Great Russell Street
London WC1*

Date *1823–52; and
later, including 1854–57*

Architects *Robert
Smirke; and others,
including Sydney Smirke*

The world's pre-eminent collection of cultural artefacts
predates the building of its first purpose-built home
by 70 years. The immense and varied collection of
scientist Sir Hans Sloane, willed to the public, was
first shown in Montague House, an 18th-century
mansion. As more and more items arrived from British
expeditions, an ambitious programme was authorised
to erect a new museum. Smirke, one of a group of
architects inspired by the extension of the Grand Tour
to new lands, designed it in the Greek Revival style.

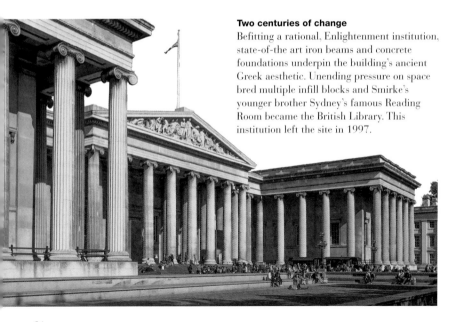

Two centuries of change
Befitting a rational, Enlightenment institution,
state-of-the art iron beams and concrete
foundations underpin the building's ancient
Greek aesthetic. Unending pressure on space
bred multiple infill blocks and Smirke's
younger brother Sydney's famous Reading
Room became the British Library. This
institution left the site in 1997.

Greek portico

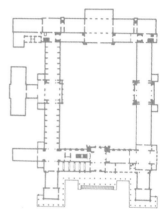

A committed Revivalist, Smirke emulated the Greek Temple of Athena Polias in present-day Turkey. On the tympanum Richard Westmacott's *The Progress of Civilisation* shows man ascending from savage to practitioner of the arts and sciences, each statue also encompassing one of the museum's interests.

King's Library (below)

George III's personal holdings, including 65,000 books, came to the museum as it was being conceived, through his son. Smirke designed towering bookcases to house this material. Polishing the granite columns was so expensive that no more were installed after the first four.

Original plan

Construction began with the east wing, housing the King's Library, and proceeded anti-clockwise until the demolition of Montague House could be secured and the main portico completed. Each range was only one room deep, but the scale of the rooms was vast.

Polychromy (right)

Archaeological discoveries confirming that Greek buildings were colourfully painted inside and out led Sydney to initiate a scheme for the entrance hall using guilloche (two braided bands) and Greek key (so called from its shape) decoration in red, blue, yellow and white. This was recently reinstated.

Park Village West & Park Village East

Location *Albany Street London NW1*

Date *1824–30*

Architects *John Nash, James Pennethorne*

Art and artifice

As with his *via triumphalis*, Nash gave considerable thought to views. The north side of the Park was left open to the hills of Hampstead and Highgate, extending the illusion of country-side. The front and back garden miniaturised this idyll.

Part of the Nash Route (page 60), the two 'villages' laid out between the imposing residences of Regent's Park and the working-class market to the east deserve separate consideration for the crucial influence they had on the century of suburban development that followed. The aspirant middle classes were rejecting the uniformity of inner-city Georgian housing, yet unable to afford mansions. Nash and his successor Pennethorne's hierarchy of types – terrace, semi-detached, villa – in styles ranging from Neoclassical to Gothic, many in their own grounds, addressed this.

Comfortable terrace

Compact and efficient, the terrace remained but when reduced to two floors and given projecting bay windows, a defensive dwarf wall and a welcoming porch, it became desirable once again. Classical references – the pillars and cornice – maintained a feeling of quality.

Fanciful villa

Providing a touch of individuality, buttresses, a steep gable, elaborate finials and octagonal chimney stacks actually mix Gothic and Tudor motifs. Nearby is a three-storey tower house, anticipating a similar thread of eccentricity to be found in several later estates.

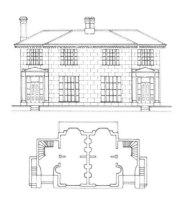

Semi-detached

A compromise, with greater privacy and space than a terrace but more affordable than a villa, this is the archetypal middle-class home. Ironically it derives from rural workers' 'double cottages', paired around a party wall to save building and heating costs.

Restrained detached

Also Neoclassical in style, with its round-headed first-floor windows and narrow coursing, the small projecting side blocks make this detached house appear even larger, echoing the wings found in grand country manor and town houses.

Royal Exchange

Location
*Threadneedle Street
London EC3*
Date *1841–44; 1883*
Architects *William Tite;
Charles Barry*

Empire state
With the new Royal
Exchange now making
a powerful architectural
group with the Mansion
House, Bank of England
and assorted commercial
palazzos, the Square
Mile was ready to play
its part at the centre of
the largest empire the
world had seen.

This, the third premises on the same site for City
merchants to transact their business within, would
have been recognised by the Exchange's 16th-century
founder, Sir Thomas Gresham. His original, based on
the Antwerp bourse he frequented in his job as trader
and royal agent, also had an open courtyard between
four arcaded wings with a floor of shops above, and
was marked by a tower. Offices now fill the upper
levels of the Exchange and luxury retailers occupy the
double-height arcade, a pleasing inversion.

Plan

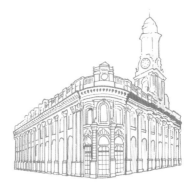

Granted an expanded plot, Tite wrapped the rectangular courtyard of previous exchanges with chambers. The resulting trapezoid conforms to the street line. He also reoriented the building toward Bank junction, the symbolic heart of the City, via a Roman Corinthian portico.

Trading places

Tite's Ionic upon Doric courtyard became the first to be roofed, in 1883. Trading ceased after 1939 but resumed in the 1980s when the London International Financial Futures Exchange moved in. Two extra (Corinthian) storeys, a refit and new roof followed in the next decade.

Poised façade

Moving the tower to the east balanced the new main entrance and completed the realignment. The curved corners are unusual and attractive. The mixture of architectural styles – Baroque, Classical, French Second Empire – became representative of the forthcoming generations.

Famous tenants

Occupiers included the only two firms authorised to transact marine insurance, Guardian Assurance and Royal Exchange Assurance, who later merged and now part-own the building, and Lloyd's, who moved from a palatial suite to their own building in 1928.

GEORGIAN STYLE

Georgian architecture was aimed firmly at the middle classes – professionals, entrepreneurs and civil servants. The City and Westminster therefore continued to attract new buildings, but they were of new kinds: blocks of offices, places to shop and trade and institutions dedicated to culture or ceremony. Housing of all types, sometimes built in new locations, catered for this discerning clientele.

① St George, Bloomsbury
Bloomsbury Way, WC1
page 40

② St Martin-in-the-Fields
Trafalgar Square, WC2
page 42

③ Old Admiralty
Whitehall, SW1
page 44

④ St John, Smith Square
30 Smith Square, SW1
page 46

⑤ Chiswick House
Burlington Lane, W4
page 48

⑥ Mansion House
Walbrook, EC4
page 50

⑦ Spencer House
27 St James's Place, SW1 *page 52*

⑧ Somerset House
Strand, WC2
page 54

⑨ Bedford Square
WC2 *page 56*

⑩ Bank of England
Threadneedle Street, EC2 *page 58*

⑪ The Nash Route
Carlton House Terrace to Regent's Park, SW1 to NW1 *page 60*

⑫ Burlington Arcade
Between Piccadilly and Burlington Gardens, W1 *page 62*

⑬ British Museum
Great Russell Street, WC1 *page 64*

⑭ Park Village West & Park Village East
Albany Street, NW1 *page 66*

⑮ Royal Exchange
Threadneedle Street, EC3 *page 68*

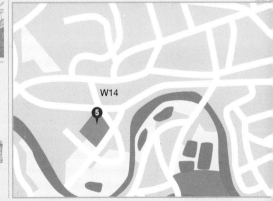

W14

⑤

Regent's Park

NW1

14

11

Hyde Park

9 13 1

WC1

12

W1

8

2

11

7

SW1

3

4

EC2 10

EC4 6 EC3

15

Battersea Park

Introduction

Power and position
The rebuilt Palace of Westminster symbolised Victorian confidence and the architectural debate of the age, with its Classical plan and Gothic Revival elevations.

No period transformed the city as profoundly as the Victorian era. London became a world city, characterised by opportunity, technology and variety and with a population supported by engineering triumphs exported around the globe. Classicism remained a popular architectural style but vied with

a revival of Gothic as the preference of the many institutional clients who dominated. These and other styles were modified endlessly, and an array of movements resulted. Many questioned if any were suitable for the new materials and entirely new types of building that began to emerge.

Palace of Westminster

When the mostly medieval Houses of Parliament suffered a disastrous fire in 1834, the competition brief for a replacement required use of the Gothic or Elizabethan style to complement the Abbey and surviving Westminster Hall. Charles Barry won, despite being best known for his Classical work, thanks to his efficient plan and partnership with the committed – even fanatical – Gothicist Pugin. He drew their joint entry and attended to every detail, from wallpaper and fabrics to furniture and fittings. The result trumpeted the Gothic Revival.

Location *Old Palace Yard, London SW1*

Date *1840–70*

Architects *Charles Barry, Augustus Pugin, Edward Barry*

Plan

The Palladian origins of Barry's scheme are clear in its logical geometry. The core functions of corridor, lobby and chamber for each House are mirrored about a central space, while cross-axes link secondary accommodation and the entrance.

High Gothic

Far above the street and so less appreciated than the sound of its famous bells, the Gothic detail of the Clock Tower is still intricate. Miniature flying buttresses, corbels, finials, gargoyles, coloured glass and a Latin inscription are all present.

Inherited ornamentation

The State Opening of Parliament is mounted in the more lavishly finished Lords. The monarch uses a throne by Pugin, closely patterned after the Abbey's genuinely Gothic 14th-century Coronation Chair. The intense, gilded decoration, carried over into its compartmented canopy, is largely heraldic.

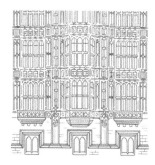

External treatment

Along the west façade, three- and four-light windows alternate, the first coinciding with projecting bays. Tracery, some of which is blind, its crocketing or leaf-like tips and the arch profile are all drawn from the exterior of the Abbey's Lady chapel (page 12).

Bridgewater House

Location
*14 Cleveland Row
London SW1*

Date *1845–54*

Architect *Charles Barry*

Informal palazzo

Of clear *palazzo* form,
with each storey
differently treated, a
lack of columns and
a protruding cornice
(employed in Italy to
cast shadows on the
façade at the hottest
time of the day),
Barry's overall
conception is far richer
in ornamentation.

Barry created this great London mansion, the last of
its type, for Lord Ellesmere, at the start of Victoria's
reign and next to Spencer House (page 52). As with
Barry's earlier Pall Mall gentlemen's clubs, the
Travellers' and the Reform, the Italian Renaissance
palazzo was the model. Highly unusually, however,
this most private of buildings here had public access
– by way of a dedicated entrance and staircase –
to a gallery displaying Ellesmere's famed picture
collection, which included paintings once owned by
Philippe II, Duke of Orléans.

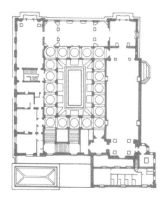

Plan

The house is centred on a roofed Renaissance *cortile* or arcaded courtyard, with the stair in a corner. Saucer-domed corridors lead to the gallery on the north side, state rooms overlooking the park, private apartments and the service wing.

Stair

The stair, with three barrel-vaulted flights around a central well, is a looser version of that found in a *palazzo*. The ceiling is coffered and flowers, foliage and other detail is deployed throughout. On the landing ahead, a saucer dome is used.

Saloon

This double-height space emerged very late in the design. The arcades are doubled, too, with paired Corinthian pilasters between each arch on the *piano nobile*. Deep coving curves the walls into the glazed roof. The extensive decoration mixes multiple historic and familial allusions.

Gallery

Though replaced by offices after the Blitz (the house is now commercial premises), the Gallery is explored for its importance in Barry's original scheme and its rarity; Hertford House, now the Wallace Collection, received its top-lit picture space 15 years later.

All Saints, Margaret Street

Location
*Margaret Street
London W1*

Date *1849–59*

Architect *William Butterfield*

Many, including Pugin and the influential Victorian critic and writer John Ruskin, believed Gothic to be a more honest, 'natural' form of architecture than Classicism. Some purists tried to continue the style directly, based on what was practised in the 14th century. As such its use in this model church for the Anglo-Catholics, a movement that encompassed many of the more dramatic elements of pre-Reformation liturgy in its worship, was a significant moment. Flaunting decorative and structural polychromy, another Ruskinian notion, All Saints also borrows from Germanic traditions.

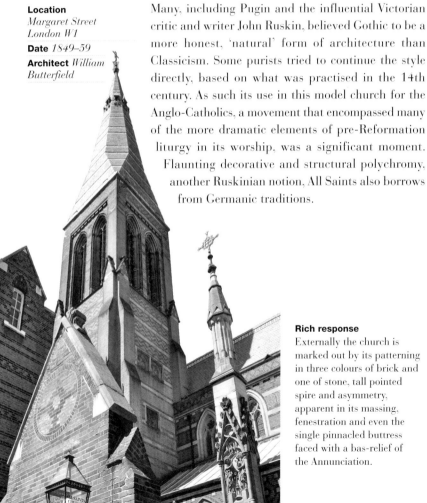

Rich response
Externally the church is marked out by its patterning in three colours of brick and one of stone, tall pointed spire and asymmetry, apparent in its massing, fenestration and even the single pinnacled buttress faced with a bas-relief of the Annunciation.

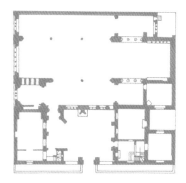

Plan

On an urban site so closely confined that no windows could be placed in either the northern or eastern walls, Butterfield was also required to fit in a choir school and accommodation for clergy. He did so in two short wings toward the street.

Pulpit

A demonstration of structural polychromy, the colours of the pulpit derive entirely from the materials from which it was made. Red, brown, grey and green stones also indicated at least four separate countries. The capitals of the short columns conform to no accepted order.

Gates

Butterfield designed the delicate gates to the chancel around the fleur-de-lis, long associated with Catholicism, and other floral motifs. The work was executed in gilt iron. The flanking walls of pierced marble – also in structural polychromy – are subtly complementary.

Walls

The interior received its finishes – of tile, paint, wood and gilt – over several decades, many of which were themselves later replaced. No surface was left untouched, by Butterfield and others. This is the dazzling tessellation above the chancel entrance.

Public Record Office

Maughan Library, King's College London

Unfulfilled proposals
Cost arguments led to delays, redesigns and cuts: a projected south range remained unbuilt. An eastward extension of Carey Street also failed to materialise, leaving Pennethorne's grand north front virtually hidden from view. Such inadequacy ultimately led to the 1972 move to Kew.

Built to bring together government documents previously dispersed across the capital, this imposing edifice shares stylistic similarities with Barry's Parliament as Gothic piers and tiered windows were the most appropriate architecture for containing and cladding the dozens of iron storage cells within. Each supported 90 tons of paper and embodied the latest fire prevention technology. The building was converted into a university library in 2001, aided by Taylor's remarkably prescient inclusion of underfloor service trenches and piping in the walls.

Location *Chancery Lane London WC2*

Date *1851–96*

Architects *James Pennethorne, John Taylor*

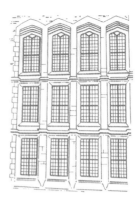

Plan

Narrow internal divisions and a long central corridor were driven wholly by the volume of material housed and the engineering of its storage system. Short wings, each with twin turrets or towers, signified the intended principal elevation.

Façade

The floor levels and narrow window bay width were determined by the limitations of the new technology of iron. The Gothic handling is more functional than Barry's, with no elaboration until the pierced parapets, decorated pinnacles and gargoyles.

Record rack

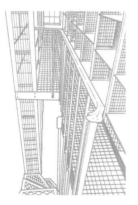

Each cell was 4.8 m (16 ft) square and 7.6 m (25 ft) high, with a mezzanine. Ventilation grilles and hot-air flues were fitted and the slate shelving – bevel-edged to minimise damage to valuable items – was adjustable. The structure, window frames and doors were all of iron.

Fireproof throughout

Load-bearing walls support iron beam floors with brick jack-arches or, in the later Taylor phases, steel beams with hollow-tile infill. The roof is also iron and the decorative 'plaster' ceiling in the entrance lobby is actually painted, welded zinc sheet.

'Albertopolis'

The Great Exhibition of 1851, conceived and promoted by Albert, the Prince Consort, was a popular and financial success, covering its costs and generating a considerable profit. Keen to embed its principles, Albert directed the establishment of an educational and cultural quarter on nearby land bought with that surplus. Under the enthusiastic management of Henry Cole, a dozen institutions slowly arose on a north-south axis. Albert died before most were completed, but from the stunning memorial his gilded statue surveys the entire site.

Baronial composition

The brick and stone Royal College of Music's end towers with *tourelles* and its tightly disposed square- and round-headed windows, some with triangular and some with segmental pediments, have the feel of a French chateau or town hall. But it was designed by a Briton, Arthur Blomfield.

Byzantine instrumental

The Royal College of Organists building, originally a music school and now a private residence, was designed by Cole's son, who contrasted its form (of the Mid-East) and façade (*sgraffito*, scratching through one layer of plaster to reveal another of a different colour) with the rest of Albertopolis.

Romanesque remains

Alfred Waterhouse's Natural History Museum epitomises the Victorian obsession with identification and classification. Hard-wearing terracotta covers the building, in Classicising panels and with a menagerie of creatures – extinct to the east, living to the west – reflecting the layout of exhibits.

Ornamental music

Designed by engineer Francis Fowke, who worked elsewhere in Albertopolis, the Albert Hall's oval brick drum with cardinal point porches closely resembles Dresden's opera house (its architect lived in London). This panel of the circumferential terracotta mosaic frieze depicts *Workers in Stone*.

Public Offices

Foreign & Commonweath Office

Location
King Charles Street
London SW1

Date *1861–75*

Architects *George*
Gilbert Scott, with
Matthew Digby Wyatt

Government machine
The building is long
and rectangular about
a large quadrangle.
Subdivision into
quarters, each with its
own smaller courtyard,
served the Offices.
There is architectural
separation, too. Each
façade is different:
two are symmetrical.
Whitehall's is articulated
with arcading
and colonnettes
(small columns).

As Britain's empire grew, a competition was staged for
a gigantic new building to hold, eventually, four
separate government departments: the Foreign, India,
Colonial and Home offices. Scott's Gothic entry
did not win but was promoted after a change of
government. A further change seemed set to reverse
Scott's fortunes when Lord Palmerston directed a
Classical solution. Scott was retained, however, and
after a much-publicised series of clashes with the
politician – who coined the term 'Battle of the Styles'
as a result – the final
form, unmistakably
Classical, was
agreed.

Park life

The India Office faced St James's Park. Its massing is more varied, featuring a belvedere or tower and a quadrant housing the Secretary of State's oval office. Coloured granite – in columns, 'apron' panels below windows and string courses – provides polychromy.

Continental drift

Quadrangle sculpture symbolises the four departments' responsibilities, something also seen toward Whitehall where this charming elephant and woman by Henry Hugh Armstead represents Asia. Parkside statues include contemporary public figures with their 'modern' clothes partly hidden under Classicising robes.

State stair

The suite of rooms built for the Foreign Office at the eastern end of the site, now named after the Locarno treaties of 1925, is served by a magnificent Roman-style staircase. The domed ceiling and coffered barrel vaults over the twin upper flights are thoroughly decorated.

Indian summer

The courtyard of Wyatt's India Office was glazed over and refloored just after the building was completed. It is now called the Durbar Court. The column orders – Doric, Ionic and Corinthian – rise as per Classical prescription. Behind the west gallery is the Council Chamber.

The Metropolitan Railway

Location
various locations
Date *1863–68*
Architects *unknown/
various architects*

All aboard

Baker Street station's
small buildings either
side of Marylebone Road
were replaced in 1911
by a single block to the
north, larger and with
rusticated arcading. It
survives as the ground
floor of Chiltern Court,
luxury flats built by the
Railway in 1930.

The Metropolitan Railway, the world's first underground
train service, began operations in London in 1863,
connecting Paddington in the west with Farringdon
in the east. The route was driven using the cut and
cover method, where earth is excavated, brick walls
and a roof where needed are constructed and the spoil
is then replaced. Trains were hauled by specially
designed steam locomotives. The line – still in use
today – was soon extended and later helped create
'Metro-Land', the Railway's development of the north-
west suburbs between the wars.

Piranesian platforms

Wells in Baker Street's tunnel walls, lined with white tiles, funnelled daylight down to the platforms and took fumes away via iron gratings. These were lost in subsequent rebuilding work above ground, but with electric traction artificial light now does the remaining job.

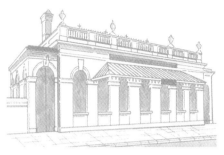

Old for new

The stations' architecture was modest though still Classical, curious perhaps given the technological advances they announced. On the initial section rendered brick simulated stone, both rusticated and ashlar (smooth-cut); on the extension, bare brick was deemed sufficient. Bayswater remains, behind clutter.

Sheltering sky

Most stations had their platforms covered by arched roofs braced by the retaining walls of the tunnels. Notting Hill Gate's reconstructed example, shown here, demonstrates how the curved iron ribs were sprung from iron corbels. Brick is laid as arcading with Tuscan pilasters.

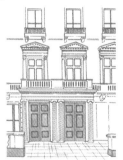

Dead end

An unusual legacy can be found in Leinster Gardens. Numbers 23 and 24 had to be demolished to allow the locomotives running below to be vented, but carefully produced fake frontages with blank doors, absent letterboxes and windows with no glass maintained decorum.

National Provincial Bank

Gibson Hall

Location *Bishopsgate London EC2*
Date *1864–65; 1878*
Architect *John Gibson*

To design its first London branch alongside a new head office, the National Provincial hired prolific bank architect John Gibson. His highly embellished, elegantly curved façade acted as a screen for a glorious, top-lit banking hall, the best of its period. Gibson returned after a dozen years to extend the frontage north by two bays, copying the first four exactly. After the bank merged with two others to form what is now the NatWest, the Hall was threatened with demolition, but it was saved and restored.

Bank statement
Genuine monumentality is evoked by the single, double-height storey, giant Composite half-columns (with Gibson's own lion volutes on the capitals and paired at the doorway) and a real depth of modelling in the elevation – that entrance is actually roofed by a barrel vault.

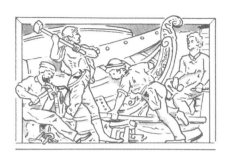

Sculptural reinforcement
John Hancock's window bas-reliefs
illustrate industries the bank financed,
for example science and agriculture, and
conveyed stability in what were troubled
times. The first set also incorporate angels,
but Charles Mabey's later pair, 'Mining'
and 'Shipbuilding', are tougher.

Standing proud
The statues above the columns – loosely
matching them one for one – represent
important business locations, plus Mabey's
two subjects once more. This is 'Wales', with
a noble St David armed and armoured
between a harp-playing bard and a miner.

Hall (left)
The largest in the City at
the time, lit by three 9.1 m
(30 ft) saucer domes with
diamond and hexagonal
glazing bars as well as the
Bishopsgate windows.
The coving is supported on
Composite marble columns,
quadrupled midway and at
each end to make arcades.

Putti panels (below)
Between the columns,
putti – a largely secular motif,
revitalised in the Renaissance
– express the Bank's funding
of fishing, farming and
textiles. At the far end of the
hall, they amusingly engage
in the extracting and smelting
of gold and its minting
into coins.

Midland Grand Hotel, St Pancras Station

St Pancras Renaissance London

Location *Euston Road London N1C*

Date *1865–77; 1866–68*

Architects *George Gilbert Scott and William Henry Barlow*

Making an entrance
Aided by the raised ground floor, the hotel announced the Midland Railway's arrival like no other. The imposing asymmetry, in plan and elevation, was generated by the competing needs of the brief but also the Gothic credo of the picturesque.

Of the many railway companies then building a terminus and hotel in the capital, none did so with more splendid results than the Midland. Barlow, their engineer, lifted the tracks over the Regent's Canal on hundreds of cast-iron columns instead of tunnelling beneath it; spaced according to the size of a beer barrel, this created convenient storage. Scott saw no contradiction between the Gothic and modernity, and visited European cities for inspiration. A triumphant restoration, repurposing and extension has reinstated the glamour of both elements.

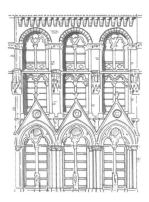

Gothic façade

Scott also blended details from several English cathedrals for his richly layered exterior. Pointed windows, cusped arches, tracery, colonnettes, arcading and triangular gables appear above the main entrance alone. The materials come from cities served by the Railway, advertising the client and structural polychromy.

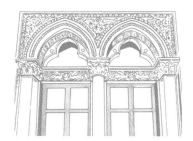

Lavish lounge

The Gothic continued inside, with arcaded quatrefoil screens and columns. The hotel's entrance hall also welcomed guests with a display of coloured stone, gilded carving – here of peacocks and vases – and patterns produced with finely cut stencilling. It is now a bar.

Honest stair

Dividing as it rises three storeys to a spectacular groin-vaulted ceiling scattered with stars, Scott's Grand Staircase flaunts rather than hides its iron structure. It is lit by two-light windows. With improving lift technology, the feature declined in popularity in such buildings.

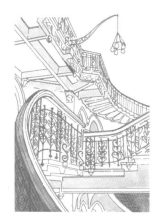

Shed rib

Pairs of curving lattice members, riveted from wrought iron, come together as pointed Gothic arches to make what was the world's largest single-span roof. Ingeniously, the platform itself acted as a tension tie, obviating the need for bracing. Openwork spandrels add interest.

Drapers' Hall

Location
*Throgmorton Avenue
London EC2*
Date *1866–70; 1898–99*
Architects *Herbert
Williams; Thomas
Graham Jackson and
Charles Reilly Snr*

The medieval livery companies of the City of London have no direct equal in Britain. Formed by, and to aid and protect, those engaged in a given trade or craft, they soon erected purpose-built halls where members could work, socialise and observe ceremony. These have been rebuilt over the centuries, as problems or prosperity demanded. The Drapers are former wool workers who bought Thomas Cromwell's house from Henry VIII. Today they are based on the same site – with its private, gated avenue – but develop property on the land they own.

Italian job

The architecture and particularly the interiors mainly resurrect two styles from 15th-century Italy: High Renaissance and Quattrocento. Both feature abundant use of coloured stones. The Court Dining Room preserves a ceiling shape from the 17th-century Hall.

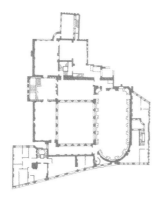

Plan

Screened by the income-generating shops, offices and eateries (added by Jackson and Reilly) that line Throgmorton Street and bridge the private Avenue is the Drapers' accommodation proper. The apsed Hall climaxes a quadrangle of Drapers' Company rooms set around a courtyard.

Entrance guardians

The entrance, itself gated, appears between those of the shops within an aedicule or surround. This comprises an open pediment bearing the Drapers' arms supported by two larger-than-life-sized atlantes or male caryatids. Their turbans refer to the Drapers' Company's trade.

Hall

The double-height Hall is an intermingling of all three architects' work. From Williams came the basic layout of Corinthian columns fronting Corinthian pilasters, doubling around the apse. Jackson and Reilly capped the room with an arcaded gallery and flat, compartmented ceiling.

Courtyard

An echo of Cromwell's house, this open space has rusticated arcading to the ground floor by Williams. The lunettes are filled with allegorical sculpture on themes including commerce and science by Edward Wyon, best known for carving medals and coins.

Smithfield Central Markets

Smithfield – 'a smooth field' – had been home to jousting, executions and also a livestock market for at least 800 years when protests over cleanliness, congestion and what we would now call animal rights prompted the creation of another piece of Victorian infrastructure: a modern, custom-built market hall. Jones conceived a pragmatic and efficient layout, whereby a central roadway divided the space into east and west wings that were then split into sectors and finally into wooden trading stalls. Jones also designed Billingsgate and Leadenhall markets.

Location
West Smithfield
London EC1

Date *1866–68;*
1879–83; 1886–88

Architect *Horace Jones*

Meat and drink

Octagonal towers crowned with copper domes and lanterns define the markets' corners and also held water for hydraulic power. Their Portland stone pavilions are packed with Classical detailing (and City of London dragons) and once contained pubs.

Stone and brick

The exterior walls of the two halls are little more than curtains, albeit with paired pilasters and round-headed blind arcading. Female personifications of major British cities flank the pediments north and south; more, wildly aggressive, dragons try to leap out of the spandrels.

Iron and glass

Grand Avenue is spanned by cast-iron frames with filigree decoration in their spandrels. Lighter varieties outline the side aisles; both rest on foliated capitals. All this was prefabricated and assembled on site. The roof is of timber, slate and glass.

Fish and chips

Jones extended the market many times. His poultry hall burnt down in 1958 but his riveted General Market further west (for fruit and vegetables) and Annexe building (fish) survive. They are threatened by a controversial office development.

7 Lothbury

Former General Credit & Discount Company

Location *London EC2*
Date *1866–68*
Architect *George Somers Clarke Snr*

Now flats but built for a discount house or trader in financial instruments, 7 Lothbury's resemblance to a miniature Venetian *palazzo* marooned in a City street has some basis in fact: in his popular illustrated book *The Stones of Venice*, critic John Ruskin drew connections between that city's success and the honest labour of craftsmen as reflected in its Gothic architecture. This is one of several more individualistic buildings put up amongst the standard Victorian commercial stock – another is the fantastically gabled 33–35 Eastcheap.

City palace

A profusion of gestures from several ages and styles is combined by Somers Clarke into a coherent and attractive whole. The marble discs on the façades, flared chimneys and projecting cornice with stepped brackets are all strongly Venetian features.

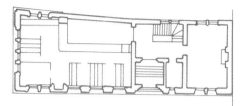

Plan

As built, the ground floor had a clerks' office, managers' rooms, porter's lodge and day-lit staircase. Remarkably the elaborate doorway was moved in 1910, presumably for increased status, from the longer but less visible Tokenhouse Yard frontage, which was then seamlessly remade.

Sphinx

The first floor window has thick stone tracery and a balcony with pierced, octofoil balustrading. It is supported by a row of very buxom sphinxes gripping shields in their claws, leading in the past to the building being described as Moorish.

Frieze

High above Lothbury a carved stone relief by medievalist James Redfern depicts steam power being handed by *Progress* to wind-tossed sailors, a farmer struggling with a plough pulled ('off-screen') by animals and a half-submerged miner draining a shaft by weighted bucket.

Doorway

Within a curved surround of alternating pink and white stones, three levels of recessed arches each have a differently moulded archivolt or underside. The full-height columns are connected by a frieze that continues the foliation of their capitals.

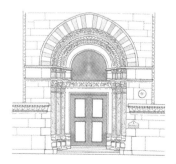

St Thomas' Hospital

Hospitality

Currey's realisation of these theories within sight of Parliament was a major landmark, literally and in hospital planning terms. A ventilation system involved shafts buried in the walls and valve-controlled zinc tubing to extract stale and introduce fresh air.

Displacement from Southwark by the expanding railway network meant this centuries-old institution was one of the first to respond to the sanitary reforms advocated by Florence Nightingale, who funded a national nursing school on the new site. Wards were treated as pavilions, widely separated to minimise the spread of 'miasma' or bad smells believed to spread infection, linked by corridors and airing courts. Currey, required to respect the Palace of Westminster across the Thames (page 74), rendered them as a series of Venetian *palazzos*. Half survived wartime bombing, but are dominated today by a white-tiled tower.

Location *Westminster Bridge Road London SE1*

Date *1868–71*

Architect *Henry Currey*

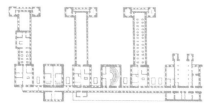

Plan

Six narrow ward spurs (half are shown here) were each spaced a full 38 m (125 ft) from their neighbours. Toilet towers are attached to the river ends. The similar positioning of the spinal teaching blocks is also visible on this upper floor-level plan.

Pavilion

Currey's Italianate theme is evident from the superimposed (stacked) arcades, paired columns and pediments. Red Fareham brick is enlivened with stone quoins, string courses and so on. The complex is therefore aligned with Parliament through its massing, rhythm and skyline rather than its detail.

Turret

Rising from the roofs of each pavilion's towers, originally between four stone pinnacles, are square-based turrets. A truncated pyramid is surmounted by a two-bay arcade that is itself crowned with a concave roof. The dainty ironwork is superb.

Air

The exact causes of infection were as yet unknown, but fresh air outdoors was recognised as vital for health. Terraces overlooking the Thames were used for 'sitting out' patients, especially children. Joseph Bazalgette's epic sewerage works, prompted by the 'Great Stink' a decade before, were already underway.

Law Courts

Royal Courts of Justice

Street view

A tower, tall and square; a few that are shorter, and adorned with circular projecting turrets; two that are polygonal, with staircases in their angles; stretches of repeated bays. A casual stroll past the Strand frontage suggests individual buildings in similar styles, serendipitously adjacent.

Street designed local churches and vicarages before securing this exceptional civic project to bring together the upper-tier civil courts of England and Wales (and, now, the criminal division of the Court of Appeal). An architecturally serious yet extravagant Gothic Revival piece, its fairy-tale roofline of towers, fleches, gables and chimneys was a knowing decision by Street, who calculated that ground level here matches the courtyard in front of St Paul's Cathedral, on its own hill to the east. Many extensions have subsequently filled the generous original site.

Location *Strand London WC2*

Date *1868–82*

Architect *George Edmund Street*

Plan

Street met the fundamental challenge of segregating conflicting parties (jurors, judges, witnesses and litigants). Each courtroom is accessed by its own spiral stair from the Great Hall; multiple other entrances are provided for different users. Clerks' rooms wrap around the outside.

Entrance window

One window beside the main door summarises Street's dedication. Two lancets or single lights, each finely shafted, sit within a pointed-head arch whose apex is filled with a sexfoil light. To its left, a gabled empty niche atop a shaft makes the external corner.

Bespoke brick

After the commanding Portland stone Strand side the other elevations are quieter with their planes of red brick, but this is set off by stone banding of varying widths and chequer work, both of real precision and complexity.

Great Hall

From the outside and within, this nave-like space shows Street's ecclesiastical bent. Recessed doorways between continuous blind arcading line the lower portion; grouped columns of varying diameter lead up to the rib-vaulted roof. The end balconies are original.

Bedford Park

Suburban spring
The search for a suitable aesthetic that avoided the cold harshness of Classicism and the ecclesiastical associations of the Gothic finally found its answer in the somewhat confusingly-named Queen Anne style, a soft, relaxed mixture of old English and northern European motifs.

The first speculative suburban development in a rural idiom, laid out by merchant Jonathan T. Carr in the grounds of the old Bedford House, is a key moment in English domestic planning and architecture. Usefully located next to the newly opened Turnham Green railway station, smaller houses (manageable without servants) in an innovative, homely style appealed to a new middle class of self-made businessmen seeking the individualisation they felt Georgian housing lacked. A pioneering local preservation campaign from 1963, years before the first conservation areas, secured its protection.

Location
Turnham Green
London W4

Date *1875–86*

Architects *Edward
William Godwin, Coe &
Robinson; William
Wilson; Richard Norman
Shaw; Edward John
May; Maurice Adams*

Pretty plan
Straight roads
converging on a new church, a pub and a row
of shops, built adjacent to the station, formed
the armature; threading gently curved or
kinked side streets around and between
mature trees added the scenic touch.
Junctions were highlighted architecturally.

Looking forward (below)
Bedford Park's language of bay
windows stacked or bracketed with
closely-mullioned lights, moulded
gables and pleasing asymmetry
informed 60 years of suburbia.
Elimination of the basement and
dwarf walls with wooden fences
instead of Georgian iron railings
also led the way.

Desirable residence (left)
It was the Park's modestly sized but
comfortable semi-detached houses that
came to define future private house design.
The earliest were by Shaw, whose tile-hung
gables and bays, massive chimney stacks
and inset semicircular window lights were
copied by his successors.

Brick borrowings
Many details were taken from
17th and 18th-century buildings,
chiefly those executed in brick.
Here a porch is marked out on
the façade by a lugged architrave
with broken, segmental pediment.
More eclecticism referenced the
Dutch and Flemish vernacular.

Tower Bridge

Location
*Tower Bridge Road
London SE1*

Date *1886–94*

Architects *Horace Jones,
George D. Stevenson
(architects), John Wolfe
Barry (engineer)*

London's gateway

Though a cautious
response to the vexed
question of how to
present new typologies,
increased trade and
the growth of railway
commuting made
Tower Bridge an
immediate operational
success. A century
would pass before
any bridge was
erected further
downstream.

Winning a competition for a new Thames crossing between the City and south bank through which tall-masted ships could still access the Upper Pool at London Bridge, Jones's bridge combined two spans on the suspension principle with a centre section using opposed drawbridge-like bascules. The steel towers were structural, and allowed pedestrians to cross above the roadway when it was open. Proximity to the Tower of London forced Jones to cover this advanced technology with brick, changed to stone after his death. Regardless, the result is world famous.

Under the skin

Four octagonal riveted steel columns form each tower, braced diagonally and connected at four levels. The suspension 'chains' for the outer roadways are in truth rigid assemblages. They pass over the towers and are joined through the high-level walkways.

Ancient garb

Weather protection aside, the bridge would function perfectly without its stone casing but arrow slits, crenellations and rustication harmonised with the Tower. Gothic plate tracery, vertically oriented with trefoil lobes, polygonal turrets and pinnacles assisted, while remaining 'current'.

Hidden power

The adjacent brick building, unassuming though still with pointed arches, housed the hydraulic system. In quiet periods a steam engine pumped water into a cylinder, raising a heavy weight. Gravity then kept the water in this accumulator under pressure, storing power for quick release.

Unexpected gargoyle

This stone dragon, probably a reference to the City of London that commissioned the bridge, looks as surprised to be perched at the top of a modern construction of steel, hydraulics and electricity as many critics were to see such an achievement cloaked.

Boundary Street Estate

Location *Arnold Circus London E2*

Date *1890–99*

Architects *various architects*

The two quite opposed definitions of 'estate' are exemplified by the seamless continuation of London's Great Estates by the aristocracy and private speculators after Victoria came to the throne and the dependence on charities, philanthropic donors or the church for public or social housing for another half-century. Only in 1890, the year after Charles Booth's poverty maps exposed the horrors of the slums and the formation of the London County Council, did Boundary Street – sitting between two parishes – became the first council estate in the country.

Mass movement
Wealthy Victorians isolated themselves from the city they had invented in illusory pastoral idylls. The later garden suburbs idealistically aimed at accommodating all classes but failed. At Boundary Street, increased rents meant almost all of the original residents were priced out.

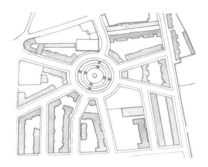

Estate of the art

A grid scheme having been rejected, the final plan radiated wide tree-lined roads from a circus, its central, mounded garden made from demolition rubble. Courtyard blocks named, possibly rather insensitively, after Home Counties towns on the Thames hugged the street line.

Variegation

Sophistication is achieved economically with brick, in a palette of sympathetic colours – pink and orange here on Hurley House – for banding and patterns and abundant if minimal Classical detailing. Such recesses, cornice, frieze and tympanum are freely combined with shaped gables elsewhere.

Surrey side

Most impressive of the more decorative blocks, the concave front of Chertsey House faces Arnold Circus with twin shallow oriel windows flanking a flat centre, and two wings flanking those. The brick banding, widening across the façade and up it, is excellent.

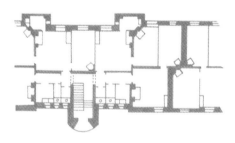

Not all mod cons

Superficially suggesting affluence from afar, blank walls abutting the pavement without the mediation of an area or garden make plain the true nature of these dwellings. Flats used open fires; many had no bath or wash basin and shared lavatories on access landings. There was a laundry block.

The Trafalgar Square Theatre

The Duke of York's Theatre

Location
St Martin's Lane
London WC2

Date *1891–92*

Architect *Walter Emden*

Victorians, less staid than commonly supposed, liked to be entertained and an explosion of venues serviced this craving. Exhibition buildings, music halls and concert halls sprang up; theatres were especially popular. In later years many more of these appeared along the new streets pushed through by the Metropolitan Board of Works such as Shaftesbury Avenue and Charing Cross Road, encouraged also by a rise in respectability of the art form (banished to Southwark in Shakespeare's time) and fire-safety improvements.

Programme
With many houses to fill, producers, companies and writers had plenty of chances to fail as well as succeed. The opening production at the Trafalgar Square Theatre was not a hit. Later it reopened under new management.

Safety curtain

Reticence best characterises Emden's Italianate façade, originally finished in bare brick save for the rusticated round-arched ground floor and first-floor loggia or open-air passage of Ionic columns. These continue as pilasters at its ends and across to the side elevations.

Downstage (right)

With more than 1,200 seats, the pit, dress circle, upper circle and gallery had many routes of escape to the outside, explaining the space devoted to staircases. Dressing rooms were isolated in a separate block connected to the stage by iron passageways.

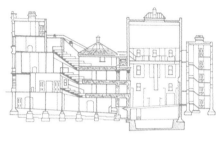

Upstage

Across foyer and offices, auditorium, stage and fly tower and dressing rooms, Emden – who designed many theatres and, later, cinemas – incorporated automatic iron doors, electric light, lavatories, steel and concrete floors, sprinklers, hydrants and ventilation by louvres and wall shafts.

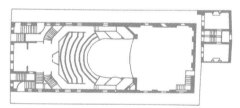

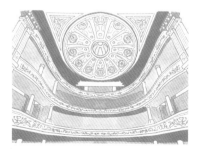

The roar of the crowd (left)

The sinuous curves of the tier fronts are notable. They and the side pillars are decorated in the Rococo Louis XV style, with plasterwork figures, swags and scrolls in cream, gold and yellow. Sight lines in Victorian theatres are generally good.

Westminster Cathedral

Location *Victoria Street London SW1*
Date *1895–1903*
Architect *John Francis Bentley*

For the Roman Catholics' much-delayed London cathedral Bentley, a practitioner of Gothic architecture, was instructed by the new cardinal, Herbert Vaughan, to utilise a style more resonant with early Christian modes of worship. Bentley, undeterred, enthusiastically toured cities including Venice and Istanbul (formerly Byzantium) for inspirational examples of 'primitive' churches. The final design included twin towers, while his chosen materials connect to the works of Ruskin, Norman Shaw and the Arts and Crafts movement. The ornamental programme, installed slowly after both principals' deaths, includes Eric Gill's Stations of the Cross.

Byzantine development

The Byzantine clustering of turrets, towers and domes and construction in load-bearing brick and Roman-style concrete speak to Bentley's primary sources. The contrast of white stonework – in bands, chequers and other repetitions – reversed out of red brick is engrossing.

Plan

Cardinal Vaughan's requirement for a basilica, that is a church to a Roman layout, is shown in the long nave, side aisles and transepts, albeit these do not project. But Bentley also included aspects of Byzantine, centralised churches, most obviously the domed crossing.

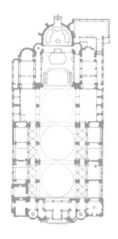

Twisting tower

Bentley's remarkable facility for transitions of form is perhaps best demonstrated at the very top of the campanile. A circular arcade takes the square base into a polygonal lantern, via blade-like buttresses of brick. The stone detailing facilitates this by leading the eye.

Faithful chapel (below)

Only two of the chapels closely correlate with Bentley's recorded intentions. That dedicated to St Gregory and St Augustine celebrates the bringing of Christianity to England. Portraits and detail are executed in mosaic, with the rest sheathed in marbles chosen by the architect.

Half full?

Almost entirely bare when services began, since a staged decorative scheme was always planned, Bentley's wish for marbled walls and mosaic ceilings is still only partly satisfied. The uncompleted space does, though, highlight the Cathedral's eastern leanings and its multiplex structure.

Location Map

Two majestic institutions, one secular and one spiritual, mark the beginning and end of this broad survey of what was an astonishingly fruitful and diverse time in London's architecture and development. Groundbreaking ways of living and working were still based in the two centres but now branched out to new districts – the suburbs. Great engineering ran beneath all, but not always invisibly.

1 Palace of Westminster
Old Palace Yard, SW1
page 74

2 Bridgewater House
14 Cleveland Row,
SW1 *page 76*

3 All Saints, Margaret Street
Margaret Street, W1
page 78

4 Public Record Office
Maughan Library, King's College London, Chancery Lane, WC2, *page 80*

5 'Albertopolis'
Queen Anne's Gate, Cromwell Road and Exhibition Road, SW7 *page 82*

6 Public Offices
Foreign & Commonwealth Office, King Charles Street, SW1 *page 84*

7 The Metropolitan Railway
Various locations
page 86

8 National Provincial Bank
Bishopsgate, EC2
page 88

9 Midland Grand Hotel
St Pancras Renaissance London & St Pancras station, Euston Road, N1C *page 90*

Hyde Park

Turnham Green

W4

SW7

10
Drapers' Hall
Throgmorton Avenue,
EC2 *page 92*

11
**Smithfield Central
Markets**
West Smithfield, EC1
page 94

12
7 Lothbury
EC2 *page 96*

13
St Thomas' Hospital
Westminster Bridge
Road, SE1 *page 98*

14
Law Courts
Strand, WC2
page 100

15
Bedford Park
Turnham Green, W4
page 102

16
Tower Bridge
Tower Bridge Road,
SE1 *page 104*

17
**Boundary Street
Estate**
Arnold Circus, E2
page 106

18
**The Trafalgar Square
Theatre**
St Martin's Lane, WC2
page 108

19
**Westminster
Cathedral**
Victoria Street, SW1
page 110

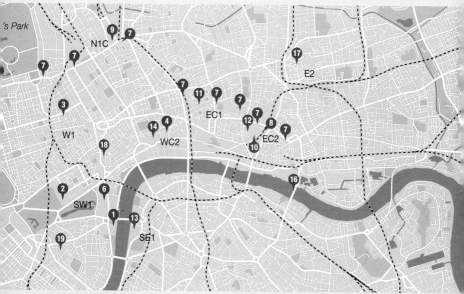

Introduction

Buoyed by the ever-growing monetary benefits of Empire and driven by the need to maintain it, the two decades of London's architecture following the death of Queen Victoria are characterised by an oversized, almost bombastic sense of scale and detail. Buildings large and small aspired to monumentality and new technology

was widespread. Having comprehensively won the 'Battle of the Styles' Classicism ruled, although it was still capable of interpretation. The individuality this produced and the wider hints of what was to come that are detectable towards the end of the period essay confidence but also change. The capital was at its zenith.

Central Criminal Court

Location *Old Bailey London EC4*

Date *1900–07*

Architect *Edward William Mountford*

One of the most famous buildings in the country, this replaced its predecessor and also one of the most feared, the awesome Newgate Gaol. The new courthouse – Neo-Baroque, with powerful gestures and high-quality materials – embodies the amplification of each architectural style that occurred at the turn of the century. It retains fascinating links to the City of London, visible in its staffing, ritual and accommodation and the line of Roman wall that it follows. And while justice may be blind, the famous figure atop its dome is not.

Criminal mastermind
Typically Edwardian, the scale and boldness of Mountford's massing and detail is nevertheless appropriate here. The rusticated base is raised and of double height. Above, channelled stone and blocky Gibbs window surrounds set off a screen of giant columns and pilasters.

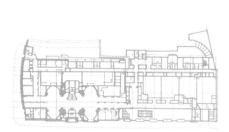

Plan

A generous lobby has four deep apses.
Opposite the original entrance is an Imperial
stair. Common in Beaux-Arts planning, it
divides for its upper, return flights which are
often narrower. This facilitates the flow of
people by dividing them, too.

North and south

A gentle bow announces the building along
historic Newgate Street, and turns the
corner. The symmetry of the west front today
is misleading; another seven bays, illustrated
here, were lost in the Blitz. The domed tower
is therefore central to neither axis.

Guardian angels

The rich compositions flanking the screen
climax at the roofline. Flowing from each
open pediment are Frederick William
Pomeroy's figures, one with sword and open
book, the other with quill and closed book.
His *Fortitude, the Recording Angel and
Truth* menaces the old entrance.

Great Hall

On the first floor a dome, supported on
pendentives decorated with Pomeroy's
allegorical sculptural reliefs and paintings by
others, lights the circulation area from which
the four original courtrooms are reached.
The similarities with cathedral architecture,
especially Wren's St Paul's, are clear.

Manor House

Location
*Marylebone Road
London NW1*

Date *1903–07*

Architects *Gordon &
Gunton*

The mansion block, an apartment building with shared staff, refuted perceptions that flats were only suitable for the working classes and established itself as a desirable compromise between suburb and town. Positioned at the edge of the city centre, porters and doormen brought elements of the lifestyle associated with the serviced terrace house or small villa while careful architectural treatment lent additional respectability. These buildings were generally of red brick, like its neighbour, but Manor House is unusual and elegant in golden sandstone. It mixes Victorian idiosyncrasy with Edwardian confidence.

New ways
Manor House's detailing is usually identified with the Arts and Crafts movement but has much in common with Art Nouveau, the contemporary but short-lived continental European equivalent. The architects began as a partnership and thrived after the First World War with commercial work.

Flat pack

An apartment is a set of rooms arranged laterally. Their layout at Manor House reflects its subtle irregularity of plan as well as elevation. One expresses the polygonal eastern corner (with its scalloped roofline turret), another the first-floor balcony and shallow bow window.

Crowning moment

Fully Classical is the apex, with open pediment, round-arched recess with oculus, niches and two types of cornice. Manor House has striking similarities to nearby Harley House by W. & E. Hunt and 37 Harley Street by Beresford Pite, both from the same decade.

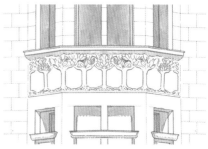

Tree house

Delicate and precise, the low relief friezes on selected bays have clear affinities with Art Nouveau motifs. Their equilibrium, however, betrays an English reluctance to depart from ordered Classical roots; indeed Art Nouveau was confined to a mere handful of buildings in London.

Revolving door

Twin porches also show Art Nouveau sympathies, with more floriated carving in their spandrels. These are, however, part of an overtly Classical structure, with a round arch between Ionic pilasters and two more of those on the return.

The Black Friar

Location
*Queen Victoria Street
London EC4*

Date *c.1905; 1917–21;
c.1925*

Architect *Herbert
Fuller-Clark (architect),
various artists including
Henry Poole, Nathaniel
Hitch, Frederick Callcott,
Farmer and Brindley*

The modern public house is, essentially, Victorian. By 1900 it was actually in decline, but this exuberant remodelling of a 19th-century original refreshes the concept. Imbued with the spirit of the Arts and Crafts movement, it also revisits with wit the period's Romanticised fascination with a medieval English past. A Dominican friary once stood on the site, and so a gently comedic community of sculpted monks is encountered working, relaxing, sleeping – everything except praying. Mottoes such as 'Haste is slow' reinforce the joke.

Opening time
The Black Friar was built in 1873–75, on a narrow, triangular plot shaped by Blackfriars Cut, the recently opened Blackfriars railway bridge and the new Queen Victoria Street. Its diagonal route, intersecting existing streets, created many such sites, distinctive to the City.

The demon drink

A green and gold mosaic band maximised the establishment's presence in its confined location. Heavy piers denote multiple entrances to capture custom from all sides but are carved with grotesque devils and merrier elves, a warning of sorts as to the dangers of intoxication.

Ale and hearty

Conversely the friars themselves advertise the pub and its wares very seductively, to judge by their postures, in a series of fretted bronze plates attached to the same piers. This amusing contradiction informs the entire decorative programme of The Black Friar.

The earth's riches (below)

Two more bronzes show the friars fishing on a Thursday and, in *Saturday Afternoon* by Frederick T. Callcott, gardening. The fruits of their labour are finished in coloured enamels. The later Grotto added alabaster, mother-of-pearl and mirrors to this exotic mix.

Snug

Warm-toned marbles, timber and copper cover the interior. Above the double inglenook fireplace is a bronze bas-relief of friars singing carols. Beyond more reliefs, the barrel-vaulted 'Grotto', under the bridge; within, monks industriously acquire a pig for the table and do their washing.

8 Addison Road

Location *London W14*
Date *1905–07*
Architect *Halsey Ricardo*

Ernest Debenham was associated with the democratic department store, another largely 19th-century innovation, but he commissioned a singular home from an architect who sought to clad the capital's buildings in brightly coloured glazed bricks, white versions of which were often employed to reflect light into gloomy courtyard offices. Famed ceramicist William De Morgan supplied extensive tiling and many other artists working in varied yet sympathetic media produced plaster ceilings, stained glass, mahogany bookcases and brass fittings to create an Arts and Crafts *Gesamtkunstwerk* or 'total work of art'.

Clean sweep
Glazed bricks in grey, green and blue echo the ground, surrounding trees and sky. Royal Doulton's Carraraware, a proprietary faience (glazed earthenware) product simulating cream marble, provided the Classicising surround of giant-order arcade and pilasters and other details.

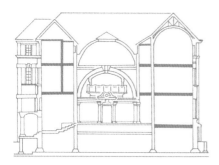

Cross-section

The central domed hall penetrates both principal storeys and the attic. Rings of rooms lead off from it. The house was well equipped, with a main and service lift, schoolroom, basement gymnasium with bath and toilet and a dozen bedrooms, each with a fireplace.

Byzantine hall

The dome, its pendentives and the triple arcades (repeating the framing device from the house's exterior) are swathed in multicoloured Venetian-style mosaic by Gaetano Meo, who also painted and was a model for the Pre-Raphaelites. The pierced marble balconies resemble Arab *musharabiyeh* screens.

Mesmeric mosaic

Greek myths, Debenham and his family and Homer's Odyssey form a not untypically eclectic subject range for the time. Ricardo, who had once designed tiles for De Morgan, had an obvious liking for the related craft of mosaic, which also has an ancient and global pedigree.

Animal magic

The circulating passages and most of the rooms, especially the bathrooms, are lined with De Morgan's tiles. They feature fish, peacocks, eagles, boar and the creatures above. All are said to have been spares from previous De Morgan commissions that Ricardo purchased as clearance stock.

Admiralty Arch

Tribute and technology
The inscription is dedicatory as are the bronze central gates, the largest in the country when made and opened only for State occasions. The Arch is partly steel-framed, and had forced air heating, fresh air ventilation via the 'chimneys' and a vacuum messaging system.

The placement and grandeur of this block are not accidental. It closes the vista from Buckingham Palace at the eastern end of the Mall, forms a ceremonial gateway to the Mall from Trafalgar Square and was part of the national memorial to the late Queen Victoria commissioned by her son, Edward VII. Practically, it provided offices and two residences for the Admiralty. The Romanesque Baroque massing and heavy detail fades on the simpler side elevations, already pointing toward the inter-war mood. Conversion to a hotel is planned.

Plan

Semicircles cleverly handle
the change of axis from
Trafalgar Square to the Mall.
The western concavity
also balances the
Victoria Memorial
ronde point outside the
Palace. The top-lit oval
staircase served the main
residence, a large light well
the offices.

Capital expenditure

Webb's engaged or attached giant-
order Corinthian columns define
the archways. Their capitals
have decorative masks between the volutes,
carved by William Silver Frith. The
spacing of the drums that comprise
the shafts matches that of the deeply
cut banded rustication.

Ready, aim...

The two sculptural figures facing the Mall
are by Thomas Brock. His *Navigation*
holds a sextant whereas *Gunnery* wears
a helm and – somewhat disconcertingly –
cradles one of the latest Armstrong artillery
pieces like a baby. Above each are
cartouches of an anchor.

First stair

A plain but impressive stair,
cantilevered from the wall, winds its
way up to apartments intended for the
First Lord of the Admiralty. After he
refused to move, the First Sea Lord
was installed in part of the suite.

Selfridge's

Location *Oxford Street London W1*

Date *1908–09; 1920–24; 1926–28*

Architects *Daniel Burnham, Francis S. Swales and R. Frank Atkinson*

After working for retailers in his native United States, Henry ('Harry') Gordon Selfridge, Snr. planned his own department store in London. He wanted large, open floors with natural light flooding in to display the maximum amount of merchandise in the most attractive manner, and brought over colleagues to help achieve this. The architectural concept is usually attributed to Burnham, who had built Marshall-Field's, the Chicago department store that was Selfridge's last place of employment, and to Swales; but it is Atkinson, a Briton, who planned the interiors. Together, they changed London shopping forever.

Speedy sales

Selfridge also used project management expertise from the United States. Steel was measured and cut off-site and delivered in sequence, colour- and number-coded for ease of assembly. Repetition in the design simplified fabrication. Phase one was completed in 12 months.

Although steel framing reduced the need for partitions, London's authorities were reluctant to relax restrictions intended to reduce the risk of fire. Atkinson's negotiations on this and doorway sizes to fully exploit the large windows led to permanent changes in the capital's codes.

Going up

Structurally, Selfridge's steel frame works with the stone façade – full separation only came to London later. The giant-order Ionic columns' spacing was academically correct but also allowed a greater expanse of glazing, as did the thin, cast-iron spandrel panels between floors.

Retail therapy

Browsing, a 'bargain basement', customer toilets and deliveries were new to Britain. Plate-glass windows were another Selfridge innovation, leading to a famous series of changing displays that continues to this day. His enthusiasm for advertising and publicity stunts was legendary.

Bigger and better

The 1928 lifts were decorated with rather erotic Signs of the Zodiac. They survive in the Museum of London. The store initially only occupied the corner of Oxford Street and Duke Street, less than half the width of today's building. Additions continued until 1973.

Royal Automobile Club

Location *Pall Mall London SW1*

Date *1908–11*

Architects *Mewès & Davis with E. Keynes Purchase*

Founded in 1897, the Royal Automobile Club soon commissioned a palatial new building as modern as its titular purpose. The Franco-English partnership of Mewès & Davis, a practised commercial firm, had already built César Ritz's London hotel and brought the same influences to bear at Pall Mall. On a structural steel frame, a Classicism of formal solemnity was essayed based on precedents from Paris rather than Greece or Italy, contrasting with Nash's Athenaeum (page 61). The latest technology was incorporated, including electricity, centralised heating and ventilation, telephones and lifts.

Road house

With motorists able to travel widely and independently, the RAC's new premises – with a formal dining restaurant, Turkish bath, gymnasium, rifle range and racquet courts plus four floors of accommodation for members, guests and staff – were more akin to a hotel than a club.

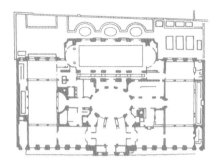

Plan

The main rooms sit on one of two axes placed at 90 degrees to each other and intersecting at the oval rotunda. The geometric planning evokes Roman and Palladian models. Three apse-like areas at ground level bring daylight to the basement swimming pool.

Luxury and leisure

The décor mixed styles and periods, including Louis IV and XV executed by French firms and reproductions of specific 18th-century English house interiors. Classical and Baroque devices, gilt and ironwork and paintings appear. The function of rooms has changed since construction.

Rotunda

Of double height, a Doric colonnade encircles its upper-level gallery. The domed glass ceiling sits at the bottom of a light well that rises four storeys to the roof. Below the ground floor the rotunda gives access to the pool via a separate stair.

Pool (below)

With anticipation heightened by glimpses from bronze-railed balconies during the approach down the stair, the Roman-influenced pool, framed by columns with diamond fish-scale patterns and lined in white Sicilian marble, does not disappoint. The tall, leaded-light 'windows' give onto the areas.

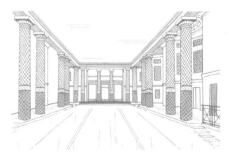

County Hall

Location
Belvedere Road
London SE1

Date *1908–33 (opened*
1922, incomplete);
1931–39

Architects *Ralph Knott;*
Frederick Hiorns and
Giles Gilbert Scott

The mammoth new riverside town hall built by the London County Council, established in 1888 as the capital's strategic authority, began as a competition-winning entry that avoided traditional symbols of civic grandiosity such as towers and domes in the interests of economy. Considerably altered for reasons of programme, aesthetics and further budgetary restraint, the final scheme's sobriety is offset by its sheer size, mirrored in over-scaled arches, plinths and statues. After 60 years' use the building now houses a hotel, apartments and an entertainment venue.

Municipal scale

The project's scope was vast, ranging from the engineering of a new concrete and granite river wall to stabilise the site to the design of the coat stands. Repeatedly extended into the 1970s, the complex ultimately comprised miles of corridors and more than 1,200 rooms.

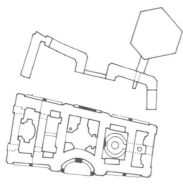

Plan

In Knott's Beaux-Arts composition the ceremonial spaces – the Chamber, main entrance and a hall – were placed on a compact east-west axis, with near-symmetrical office wings around courtyards extending either side. The hall was later deleted and its sheltering crescent moved to face the river.

Sculpture

Delays due to strikes, escalating costs and the First World War meant the figurative sculpture accompanying both early phases was very different from what Knott envisaged. Ernest Cole's allegorical groups in particular – Modernist and 'difficult' – caused controversy. Their subjects were unclear even at the time.

Façade

The Members' Entrance – set into the south façade relatively late in the design process – shows Knott's muscular Classicism in its massive granite pedestrian entrances (equine sculptures were planned on top), modelled arch and bold carving. A vaulted, Piranesian tunnel leads to the courtyard beyond.

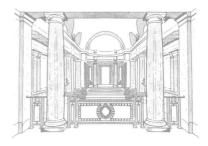

Ceremonial staircase

Austerity notwithstanding, carefully hierarchical levels of fit-out in wood panelling, plaster, bronze and marble were applied, favouring the lobbies and Members' and Chief Officers' rooms. Coupled marble columns supporting a barrel-vaulted ceiling proclaim the Principal Floor at the top of the east entrance stair.

Michelin Building
Michelin House

Location *Fulham Road London SW3*

Date *1909–11; 1912; 1922*

Architect *François Espinasse*

Carchitecture

As a result of its very specific agenda, the Michelin building is architecturally uncategorisable, though pleasantly so. Extended twice but sold in 1985, it was revived by conversion to a Conran restaurant and shop, restoration and the addition of offices.

Support for the expensive and fragile motor car quickly appeared. Michelin, the French tyre company, built a new London headquarters with drive-in service bay that was also an early example of architecture as advertisement. Every component was so co-opted, with rustication resembling the treads of tyres, pilasters with the company's intertwined initials as capitals and large faience friezes bearing its full name. One of the first corporate logos, a rejected brewery advert ('*Bibendum*' is Latin for 'drink') adapted at the Michelin brothers' suggestion, was also built in.

Faience façade

All of the Fulham Road frontage and substantial portions of the returns were faced with 'Marmo', artificial marble recently invented by Leeds-based Burmantofts Pottery. White, blue, yellow and green were used for walls, cartouches, cornices and the relief lettering.

Glass man

Three stained-glass windows feature Bibendum in poses copied from the company's posters: cycling, toasting the excellence of Michelin products and – in the most graphically radical image – kicking the tyre-treaded sole of his foot 'out' of the window toward the viewer.

Tired?

Tyres appear in three dimensions beside the arched window, stacked in diminishing diameters as glass cupolas and in the tympanum to the segmental pediments on the side elevations. Racing car victories on Michelin tyres are commemorated in pictorial tiles inside and out.

Concrete proposal (below)

Appropriately for a client at the cutting edge of technology, the building used the pioneering reinforced concrete structural framing system invented by François Hennebique in 1896. Fire-resistant, capable of carrying great weight and fast to erect, it was ideal.

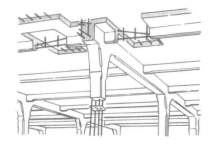

18–22 Haymarket

Formerly Burberry's

Location *London SW1*
Date *1911–13*
Architect *Walter Cave*

The new methods of sale and display popularised by Selfridge (page 126) and enabled by his brasher architecture soon spread to smaller merchandisers. Surrey-born draper Thomas Burberry, inventor of waterproof gabardine and, later, the trench coat, established a new head office and what we would today call a flagship store south of Piccadilly Circus. His architect's design opened up its frontages as far as possible, with stonework reduced to the bare minimum conducive to a broadly Classically styled building. Burberry only left the site in the early 2000s.

Retail opening

Cave took a Mannerist or more individual approach to Classicism in his detailing. Gifted with a useful corner site, he made the most of it by employing the same architectural treatment on both elevations. This brought coherence and avoided connotations of a lesser frontage.

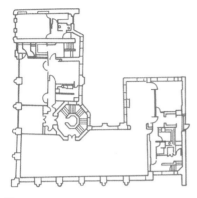

Plan

Though common as a way of preserving neighbours' rights to light, an L shape gives narrower floors that benefit from increased daylight penetration. The shop's top-lit, octagonal customer stair was wrapped around its lift; the arrangement saved space and made a dramatic feature.

Window shopping

At street level the tall entablature and widely spaced engaged Doric columns permit the maximum amount of glass, an enticing prospect for retailer and customer alike. A giant-order Ionic arcade above combines with recessed metal spandrels to imply a similarly attractive double-height upper level.

Floor display

The ground floor is shown in the opening year. The wood panelling was originally limed oak. Cave's decoration was also still Classical, but times were changing. The pilasters and compartmented ceiling are attenuated, there is no other ornamentation and the light fixtures are frankly Moderne.

Detail

The same banding is carried across the drums of the columns, the walls and the rustication on the wider pilasters that terminate each of the façades. Foliated carving, lion heads and other carving is minimal. Original lettering leaves its traces, a history retained by the new tenant.

Port of London Authority

Ten Trinity Square

Location *Trinity Square London EC3*
Date *1912–22*
Architect *Edwin Cooper*

The Port of London Authority was founded in 1908 to manage nearly 160 km (100 miles) of the Thames, particularly its commercial river traffic and associated dock systems. Its headquarters, by one of the most highly regarded architects of the day, is perhaps the apogee of Edwardian swagger, symbolically facing downstream to welcome the immense wealth being brought daily into the city. After decades as commercial offices when the PLA departed, the building is now serviced apartments, a hotel and a club.

River island
The PLA building stands at the very edge of the City – the ancient 'Liberties of the Tower' cuts across its entrance – and overlooks the 18th-century Trinity Square Gardens. New streets were laid out to its north and south.

Street block

Cooper's building is a simple quadrangle extruded upward by many storeys and with the south-east corner sliced off. A domed concrete Rotunda in the courtyard, housing a series of concentric counters for logging shipping movements, was destroyed in the Blitz.

'Father Thames'

From his shell-like apse, Alfred Hodge's evocation of the PLA's – and London's – source of prosperity points to the far-off estuary. This sentinel stands on an anchor upon a capstan, his rippling muscles and the folds of his cloak reminiscent of waves.

Towering ambition

Simultaneously colossal and intricate, the temple-like tower would be an impressive building in its own right. Two Corinthian porticos with statues signifying *Exportation* and *Produce* flank the apsed central block. Its square cap diminishes toward a shallow pyramidal roof.

Board rooms

The Board Room and Committee Rooms are typical for the period, with plaster ceilings and oak and walnut panelling. The former has carvings on the themes of Empire and world trade: each of the latter has a different Classical order.

The Quadrant

Refined vista
Blomfield's curving ranges either side of the hotel are each 12 bays wide, ensuring the balance mandated for the west side of Regent Street. After the punctuation of a passageway, an identical stretch repeats this rhythm up to Vigo Street, the Quadrant's northern limit.

Piecemeal alterations, isolated rebuilding and demolition of the colonnades following concerns over impropriety and lack of light eventually forced comprehensive redevelopment of this part of the Nash Route (page 60). The Portland stone-clad, Neo-Baroque rear elevation of the Piccadilly Hotel, which had breached the Regency stucco and scale of the southern portion in 1908, provided the model for a new Quadrant and its centrepiece, but after retailers objected to its architect Norman Shaw's arches restricting their display space, his pupil Blomfield was asked to continue the work.

Location *Regent Street, London W1*
Date *1923–28*
Architect *Reginald Blomfield*

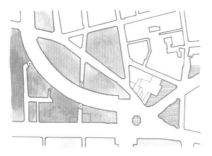

Perfecting portals

Side streets or alleys join the Quadrant at four points. By carrying over each his version of Norman Shaw's heavily rusticated semi-circular arch surmounted by columns and an upper-storey bridge, Blomfield ensured the clean line of both façades remained undisturbed.

Street life

Nash's Piccadilly Circus was first intruded upon by the cutting of Shaftesbury Avenue in 1886. Blomfield's rectilinear replacements for the County Fire Office and Swan & Edgar further eroded its purity. The Crown Estate is currently reviving the neglected blocks to the north.

Shop front (below)

Tenants' determined demands for shallow, unobstructed windows drove the replacement of Norman Shaw's arches with Blomfield's simpler, square-headed openings elsewhere. They mainly benefitted the mezzanine floors, which gained considerably more daylight. Behind these examples lies the Quadrant Arcade, by Gordon Jeeves.

Pavilions

With the southern terminations of the two Quadrant blocks, Blomfield echoed Nash's scheme – both buildings broadly follow his arcading and roofline. To the north Blomfield used splayed ends, slicing off their corners. This gave visual interest from the crossing streets and when heading south.

27–35 Poultry
Former Midland Bank

Location *London EC2*
Date *1924–39*
Architect *Edwin Lutyens, with E.G. Stevenson and executive architects Gotch & Saunders*

One of Britain's greatest architects, Lutyens designed several prestigious commercial premises in addition to his civic and domestic work. His personal friendship with the Midland Bank's chairman led to several commissions for the bank, including this new headquarters on a site acquired in a takeover. It is undoubtedly the pinnacle of the golden era of banking palaces, its magnificence a fitting end to this chapter of London's architectural story. Latterly occupied by HSBC, the Midland's successor, the building is now destined to become a luxury hotel.

Bank account

Lutyens showed tremendous subtlety and sophistication in the elevations. The rustication narrows by an eighth with successive courses, windows stretch the higher they are placed and the entire façade inches back with each smooth stone band. Doric pilasters disappear as they rise.

Plan

The Poultry site also has a narrow exposure to Princes Street. The two façades are not parallel. Lutyens's skill was to conceal this 45 degrees misalignment of axes with a pivot about the circular marble well that lit the basement safe deposit.

Sculpture

The exterior is refined and ingenious, but Lutyens also had a childlike sense of humour: above the corner mezzanines on Poultry are William Reid Dick's statues of a boy and a goose, taken from ancient Greek sources yet wittily alluding to the building's address.

Banking hall

Two storeys high, the banking hall is filled with square Corinthian columns and pilasters of green African stone with contrasting white plaster capitals. These are set against white marble walls and walnut counters. Extravagant doorcases are topped with a typically Lutyens dome and clock.

Silent partners

Suitably for a building that is the apotheosis of inter-war Classicism, the board room sits on the top floor, entered behind the arched window. A sound-absorbing quilt for the upper walls was faced with the largest tapestry ever made in England, featuring the coats of arms of British cities.

Location Map

Institutions continued to dominate during these years, with County Hall, the Port of London Authority and the Central Criminal Court all notable. Much grander places to shop, calculated to impress aesthetically and perform financially, appear in the West End, erasing a previous generation's iteration in Regent Street. Victorian eccentricity, magnified by Edwardian self-assurance, dotted surprises around the capital, including in Addison Road and Fulham Road.

1 Central Criminal Court
Old Bailey, EC4
page 116

2 Manor House
Marylebone Road, NW1 *page 118*

3 The Black Friar
Queen Victoria Street, EC4 *page 120*

4 8 Addison Road
W14 *page 122*

5 Admiralty Arch
The Mall, SW1
page 124

6 Selfridge's
Oxford Street, W1
page 126

7 Royal Automobile Club
Pall Mall, SW1 *page 128*

8 County Hall
Belvedere Road, SE1
page 130

9 Michelin Building
Fulham Road, SW3
page 132

10 18–22 Haymarket
SW1 *page 134*

11 Port of London Authority
Ten Trinity Square
Trinity Square, EC3
page 136

12 The Quadrant
Regent Street, W1
page 138

13 27–35 Poultry
EC2 *page 140*

4 W14

NW1

Regent's Park

W1

Hyde Park

SW1

SW3

Battersea Park

SE1

EC1

EC2

EC3

EC4

Introduction

The new forms of expression and construction that emerged in the Edwardian era found their locus at the design-based Exposition Internationale des Arts Décoratifs et Industriels Modernes of 1925 in Paris, from which the term Art Deco was later coined, and in the broader contemporaneous movement called

Modernism, which also began on the Continent but which eschewed decoration in favour of logic, functionality and technology. These and their offshoots informed architecture up to the war, but were very often in tension with each other and older, surviving styles as the capital struggled to find its way.

Modern life
Even interiors had many manifestations, from the joyous exuberance of Art Deco cinemas to the bare concrete of the Royal Horticultural Society's New Building.

Adelaide House

Location *London Bridge London EC4*
Date *1921–25*
Architects *John Burnet and Thomas Tait*

This office and warehouse building, the tallest ever built in London at the time, greets those crossing London Bridge from the south as a powerful and expressive gateway to the City. A minimalist, repetitive façade contrasts with the aged building it replaced and shows the belated influence of the Chicago School, while the 'Egyptian' massing and motifs manifest a wider cultural obsession of the day. The architects, sometimes constituted with others, had one of the most prolific commercial practices of the inter-war years, often also working in suburbia.

Megalith

The monumental outline, battered (sloped) piers, deeply recessed windows and Middle Eastern detail reflect then-recent archaeological advances – the discovery of Tutankhamun by Howard Carter occurred in 1922. The whole resembles a Modernist pharaoh's tomb erected by hordes of slaves on the banks of the River Thames.

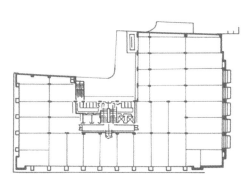

Plan

Stairs, lifts and toilets were grouped in the same position on each storey, maximising efficiency; a service core, in today's terms. This and stacking so many identical floors was new. Centralised heating and ventilation, an internal mail system and multiple telephone connections were provided.

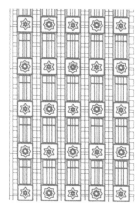

Grid

The apparent solidity of Adelaide House is misleading. As with the pioneering skyscrapers of Chicago, a steel frame lies beneath the thick stone, permitting regular fenestration and a surprisingly high window-to-wall ratio. The reduced spandrel ornamentation – stars here – is also characteristic of North America.

Roof

The big cornice shows a decisive break from Classical tradition. Shying away from the corners, undercut with fin-like dentils and with geometric reliefs beneath this, it expresses the building's 'Egyptian Deco' tendencies. Above it, staff could play miniature golf on a landscaped course.

Sculpture

Solemnity informs the bridge-level entrance, from William Reid Dick's figure to the apparent weight compressing the Doric columns. It is set within a granite plinth extending part-way up the building like a watermark. The quayside loading bay was finished in rubber in order to minimise noise.

Piccadilly Circus Underground Station

Location *Piccadilly London W1*

Date *1924–29*

Architects *Adams, Holden & Pearson with Stanley Heaps (architects), Harley Hugh Dalrymple-Hay (engineer)*

Facing a tremendous increase in passengers using their congested existing station in the heart of the West End, the Tube companies involved decided to relocate it underground with a large, planned circulation system and integrated facilities. Slow and cramped lifts were replaced by banks of escalators and the elliptical hall was designed to facilitate the flow of people between lines and streets, thanks to a network of subways. Holden went on to design many stations and the Underground's head office (see page 152).

Going underground

At pavement level the stylised Romanesque lamp standards and illuminated logo hint at the modernity below. Life-sized mock-ups were used to test the placement of these new openings and the equipment for the concourse, which sits under a steel and concrete roof.

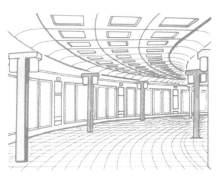

Railway rotunda

More than 50 columns in concentric circles support the road junction above. A plaster suspended ceiling (subsequently replaced with enamelled metal), shallowly coffered and corniced, minimised claustrophobia and travertine covers the walls. Shop fronts are set into the circumference and around the escalator well.

Seductive subways

Four generous passages, also lined with travertine and fitted with revenue-raising bronze-framed poster panels and display cases, lead to and from the street entrances and directly into the lower ground floors of some nearby stores. Direction signage is clear.

Columns and lights

The columns are facetted and clad in maroon *scagliola* (a marble substitute, now painted), with fluted bronze capitals. From them hang luminaires with tungsten filaments. Use of tactile, self-finished – and therefore low-maintenance – materials became common in Holden's future work for the Underground.

Hub of empire

The linear or World Time Clock is set into the wall of the central area. A thin band moves continuously, indicating the current time and hours of daylight at any location across the globe 24 hours a day. Major cities are highlighted.

Royal Horticultural Society New Building

Lawrence Hall

Location
Greycoat Street
London SW1

Date *1925–28*

Architects *Murray Easton and Howard Robertson (architects), Oscar Faber (engineer)*

Behind a plain frontage resembling a block of flats or perhaps a cinema is one of the most innovative spaces of the period. Encouraged by work in France and Germany on hangars, sports arenas and churches, reinforced concrete arches of near-parabolic form almost 18 m (60 ft) high create a lofty exhibition hall with no need for additional support. Left exposed the look was radical, while as the first of its kind it was instrumental in changing how British regulators assayed concrete as a structural medium.

Back and forth
The brick and Portland stone exterior is Neo-Georgian, then seen as reactionary. It does hark back to London's past, but also shows the incorporation of the smooth lines and gentle arcs that would become synonymous with Moderne, the softer, more accessible reading of Modernism.

Discreet decoration

A fundamental characteristic of Modernist architecture is the reduction and eventual elimination of applied ornament. The enrichments of Classicism were remorselessly targeted; any remaining sculpture was gradually flattened. This bas-relief symbolising growth under the sun's rays is typical.

Industrial cathedral (below)

The arches – set more than 6 m (20 ft) apart – define a 'nave' and the horizontal roof slabs 'aisles', which here assist structurally by resisting the outward thrust of the former. A triplet of windows in the far wall reinforces the parallel.

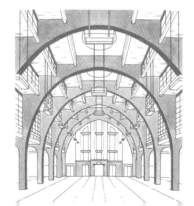

Entrance curve

Bright lobbies promoting a feeling of calmness and arranged with few obstructions and elegant logic were common in public buildings of this age. Multiple doors, mostly of glass and with slim metal frames, contribute and contrast with the imposing single portals of old.

Light fantastic

The four set-backs in the brick box containing the hall provide diffuse side lighting through extensive glazing. Rising, each is lower than the one before, following the shape of the arches. The roof and bottom tiers have skylights between each pair of ribs.

55 Broadway

Location *London SW1*
Date *1927–29*
Architect *Charles Holden*

With the new head office for the Underground Electric Railways Company of London, which ran the core of today's Tube, Holden accepted a tight, irregular site above St James's Park station and with two conceptual masterstrokes gave birth to a generous moment of urban planning and one of the city's best examples of an early high-rise. A short cut through the kite-shaped plot helped the public, while an American-inspired stepped, cruciform office block improved daylighting for its occupants and reduced overshadowing on the ground. Conversion into flats is planned.

Modern movement

Holden had inverted the street-hugging building with interior light wells in an earlier hospital design. Careful massing and restrained detail denotes Stripped Classical architecture. Planners limited 'inhabited' floors to 24 m (80 ft) above ground, so the tower's upper levels are largely empty.

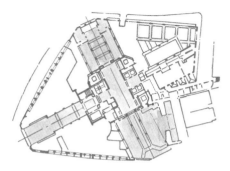

Move down inside

Broad access passages offered a way to cut off the street corner; such permeability had been common in the United States for decades. Late 1980s remodelling altered the route, formed a larger, secure office lobby around the service core and increased the shopping zone.

Connected offices

Work areas were subdivided by demountable steel partitions. Piping and fire escape stairs – vital in a tall building – occupied the wing junctions. Even the landings were liberally equipped, with a bay window seat, clock, display shelf, marble drinking-water fountain and internal mail chute.

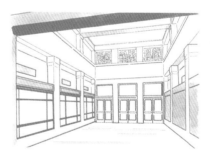

Retail revolution

The mall walls are lined with travertine. Its distinctively porous, striated texture is non-slip, making it ideal for the floor as well. Bronze fittings, clocks in an Art Deco sunburst, a coffered ceiling and lighting (many still the original features) confirm Holden's aspirations for all users.

Air supply

High above Jacob Epstein's groups *Day* and *Night* are eight figurative relief panels of the Winds, two per wing, carved by artists including Eric Gill and Henry Moore. Contained by the architecture, Samuel Rabinovitch's *West Wind* is accompanied – uniquely, wonderfully – by a gull.

New Victoria Cinema

Apollo Victoria Theatre

Location *Wilton Road, London SW1*

Date *1928–30*

Architect *E. Wamsley Lewis with executive architect W.E. Trent*

Cinemas sometimes merged the International Style, the more rigorous strand of Modernism, with the populist optimism of Art Deco and its focus on decoration. The severe exterior of this capacious 'super cinema', built by a chain just as talking pictures arrived, dissolves into a fantasy interior that borders on the kitsch. Fortunately, the complex circulation – necessary in a venue that is partly underground and has a central foyer accessed from parallel streets – is strictly and reassuringly rational.

March of time

With polygonal engaged columns of black marble topped with electric lamps and fluting to the stone cladding behind, the verticality of the entrances – restored some years ago – mark the building out as a formal tower would have done previously.

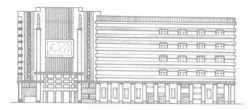

Streamlined Moderne

In contrast the façades – identical, save for mirror-imaged entrances to the foyer – generate a pronounced horizontality from their full-length projecting ribs, narrowly set at half-storey intervals. Strip windows in these otherwise blind elevations add to this emphasis and typify the age.

'Mermaid's heaven'

The idiosyncratic and exotic auditorium has pilasters fountaining into giant scallop shells as they rise, to be met by glass stalactite lights coming down from the ceiling. The original concealed lighting scheme, with cycling washes of colour, motivated the current digital system.

Double take

Flanking the Wilton Road entrance are surprising, witty frieze-like reliefs by Newbury Abbot Trent, sculptor cousin of the executant architect, in which the same cinema audience of contemporary and Classically dressed (or undressed) figures watches and reacts to a romance followed by a thriller.

Nautical notions

Several Moderne buildings share styling cues with the ocean liners of the day: architects worked on both. Inside this sleek, symmetrical exterior lurk aquatic creatures and fronds. Trent's panel personifying cinema – she dances with a 'ribbon' of celluloid – is in the essentially intact foyer.

Hay's Wharf Head Offices
St Olaf House

Location *Tooley Street London SE1*

Date *1930–32*

Architect *H.S. Goodhart-Rendel*

With some of the functionality and architectural spirit of the Venetian *palazzo*, this riverside jewel box of a building also blends the dynamism of German Expressionism and the presence and practicality of the British warehouse. The materials and the stylish interiors, many of which survive, also characterise the Modern movement. It was built by the Hay's Wharf Company, which managed a significant stretch of the dockside along the Upper Pool, but the building is now part of a private hospital.

Office block

To maximise floor space but keep the quayside free, the Thames-facing block is raised on granite columns. Chamfered storeys give the impression of a floating white cube, although the sloping attic actually lit drawing offices. The gilded sculptural surround dominates.

Maximum packing

The landward buildings are narrower, to ensure good light levels in the offices. Stairs sit behind Expressionist staggered windows and a black-and-gold mosaic of St Olaf, King of Norway, commemorates the help he gave King Ethelred to defend the City of London against the Danes in 1014.

River front

Sculptor Frank Dobson worked in Doulton faience, metal and granite to frame the canted windows and balconies of the double-height Board Room and Directors' Common Room. Three large reliefs illustrate *Capital*, *Labour* and *Commerce* and 36 smaller pieces depict the *Chain of Distribution*.

Board games

The triple-bay division of the river façade is carried into the Board Room behind, via polished trim on the coved ceilings and walls containing flush illumination. The central strips die away as the rear wall drops incrementally to single-storey height.

Entrancing

On the street side a sheltering *porte cochère* or undercroft with an illuminated, faceted glass ceiling leads to the lavishly decorated entrance. The gold-incised lettering above the doors is original, accompanied by coats of arms. Zigzag decoration, also on the doors, evokes rippling water.

Broadcasting House

Location *Portland Place London W1*

Date *1930–32*

Architects *G. Val Myer (architect), Raymond McGrath (decorative consultant and some interiors), other interiors by various architects*

The BBC's first purpose-built home was as advanced for the time as its Television Centre would be a generation later. A new building type, this radio city was packed with sophisticated audio and transmission equipment, technical and dressing rooms and offices.

The windowless, artificially conditioned studios for voice and music, drama and news were designed by other architects working to McGrath, a practitioner in his own right. All areas featured streamlined curves, pastel colours, inventive glass usage and integrated lighting, sometimes behind false windows.

Portland place

Critics felt Myer's Portland stone block overwhelmed the locale, though its slow convexity does respect the route laid out by Nash more than a century before (page 60). A massive 'tower' of load-bearing brick within isolated the studios from external and internal noise.

Geometry

The lobby occupies the 'prow', originally intended – like much of the ground floor – for retail. Myer used columns on one side to outline a more aesthetically pleasing semicircular space within the elliptical shell. The controversial extension of 2013 forms a U with his building.

Radio Ariel

Shakespeare's spirit character Ariel from *The Tempest*, whose name may derive from 'air', appears in three façade bas-reliefs and a statue, where his master Prospero is also present. The fiercely religious Eric Gill carved them, here interposing his more biblical interpretation.

Concerto

In the balconied, underground Concert Hall, attention was focused on the stage by a boldly expressed ceiling and coffered piers. Between these are Classical bas-reliefs by Gilbert Bayes. An organ was fitted. The Hall later became the Radio Theatre.

Reception

Despite Myer's efforts the lobby is asymmetrical, given the difficult plan. Gill's sculpture *Sower*, representing the potential of broadcasting, is today trapped behind the glass security screen that divides the space. Above is the Council Chamber and above that the Director General's office.

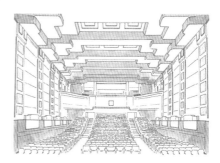

Daily Express Building

120 Fleet Street

Location *Fleet Street London EC4*

Date *1930–33*

Architects *Owen Williams (architecture, engineering) with Ellis & Clarke, Robert Atkinson (entrance hall)*

The *Daily Express* brought the familiar treatment for suburban factories during this period to the City, with a spectacular front concealing a utilitarian rear. Dramatic, curved glazing, flush and half black, sheaths Atkinson's 'Jazz Deco' lobby and renowned engineer Owen Williams's reinforced concrete structure, which forms the vast basement printing hall and stepped-back tiers of offices above. An immaculate restoration in 2000 removed a crude extension to the east and completed the corner to the original design, but the lobby is now generally screened from view.

Curtain wall
Considered to be Britain's first building clad only in glass, Williams wanted complete transparency with the concrete exposed, but the client refused and Vitrolite, an opaque, pigmented glass made by Pilkington Brothers, was employed for the spandrels. Structure and finish were, though, finally independent.

Free span

The size of the presses drove a requirement for column-free space. Williams's solution was a portal frame spanning almost 18 m (60 ft)

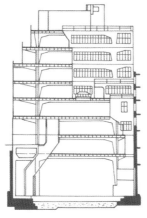

between just two supports. It also cantilevers to the west, providing more office space above a recessed loading bay. Five portal frames form each storey.

World reach

Eric Aumonier sculpted the two epic gilded plaster murals, *Britain* and *Empire*, depicting in almost infinitely absorbing detail the home nation and her colonies engaged in industry of all kinds. The hall is now used for receptions and the like by its new owner.

Advertisement

Callers used Betty Joel-designed furniture, now lost, to place advertisements amidst a sculpted silver-leaf ceiling with huge pendant boss, walls of black Belgian marble and travertine and a multicoloured wave-patterned floor, these all saved or recreated. Atkinson was a noted architect himself.

Circulation revolution

The elliptical stair is made from concrete, poured into wooden shuttering or moulds in situ and then finished in *terrazzo*, marble chips in resin polished when set. During the restoration original lift shafts, too small now, were reused as service ducts.

Senate House

Location *Mallet Street London WC1*

Date *1931–37*

Architect *Charles Holden*

This colossal, grave edifice was built by the University of London as the ceremonial and administrative centrepiece of its new campus. The building is of Portland stone and brick, though the weight of a million books meant a steel frame was needed in the library tower, which – at 64 m (210 ft) – made Senate House the tallest building in London after St Paul's. The austerity of the Stripped Classical exterior – unlike in Holden's other early buildings, plinths for statues remain empty to this day – contrasts with the coolly luxurious spaces within.

Stripped ease

The Stripped Classical style derives its name from the use of Classical elements that are often implied rather than explicit: narrow, closely set windows with depressed spandrels read as continuous voids, the stone walls in between as columns or piers.

Spinal plan

The University's vision was to extend north over three decades, continuing the model of courtyards either side of a 'spine'. A shorter version of the tower would have terminated the scheme, although funding problems were to do so in reality.

Vestibule (above)

This low entrance, unusually open to the outside, has fluted corner pilasters with vestigial bases and capitals. It is lined with travertine, and bronze uplighters on the walls lend a sense of formality, even of ritual.

Hall

Within, a double-height circulation lobby between two large meeting halls holds an impressive central staircase to the first-floor ceremonial circuit. Only three materials are used: bronze, travertine and plaster for the ceiling, whose compartments are patterned after London plane trees.

Restraint

Holden's restriction of decoration to small details – some stained window glass, brass insets to wood panelling – foreshadows the arrival of the purer Modernism. Electricity lit and heated the building and provided moveable bell and telephone points.

Peter Jones

Location *Sloane Square London SW1*

Date *1932–37; 1939*

Architects *William Crabtree, J.A. Slater and A.H. Moberley (executive architects), C.H. Reilly (consultant)*

Welsh retailer Peter Rees Jones moved to London and then to this site, where he built a large, red-brick store on its northern fringe in 1889. Competitor John Lewis bought the concern after Jones's death and between the wars turned to the John Lewis Partnership's recently hired research architect for a new design for the store. Crabtree had worked in the United States with Modernist architect Raymond Hood, but the primary influence was that of continental Europe, specifically the Chemnitz branch of the Schocken department store chain by the German Erich Mendelsohn, completed two years previously.

Super store
This steel-framed, curving glass curtain wall was something new. The subtleties of plan in the first phase include the gentle corner swell and the two small steps forward in the façade overlooking Sloane Square. Phase one stopped just down Kings Road.

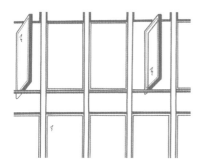

Supple glass

Reilly, dynamic leader of the Liverpool School of Architecture, admired Mendelsohn's design but Crabtree's was far lighter, with larger windows and spandrels of opaque glass rather than stone. Thin mullions at 1.2 m (4 ft) centres varied the visual rhythm, and at a human scale.

Double curve

Sheets of storey-height plate glass joined only by the thinnest possible vertical bars formed a continuous shop front, with contents and shoppers protected by a similarly prolonged cantilevered canopy. Curved ceilings reflected light onto the goods being shown. Frilly blinds were a traditional hangover.

Functionally superior

The debt owed to Chemnitz is also seen on the rectilinear Symonds Street façade, with its very large display window across the ground floor, solid 'bookend' and upper-level setbacks, where, as with the rest of the store, a bronze screen balustrade follows the perimeter.

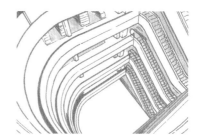

New season

In a 2004 refurbishment one of the two internal light wells was remodelled with curved floor edges and new escalators in a single, continuous circulation route through all storeys. Services were also improved. Sadly the rooftop swimming pool planned in 1932 was not installed.

64 Old Church Street

Location *London SW3*
Date *1935–36*
Architects *Erich Mendelsohn and Serge Chermayeff*

House arrest

In red-brick Chelsea, the Cohen house is startling even today, albeit reassuringly readable. The upper windows light the back stair and staff bedrooms, the much larger glazed expanse the hall, main stair and landing. Bathrooms lie behind the two horizontal windows, right.

The villa was a key trope of the Modern movement, whether Le Corbusier's Villa Savoye or Mies van der Rohe's Villa Tugendhat, but Britain had held it at a certain distance, deeming the flat roof, white walls and staring windows aesthetically, socio-politically and practically inappropriate. Such examples as were built in London, largely by émigrés fleeing mainland Europe, were mostly confined to the suburbs. The centrally sited Cohen house (so called after the building's first owner, publisher Denis Cohen) is rare, along with its much-altered neighbour.

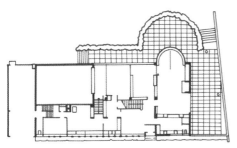

'A machine for living in'

Le Corbusier's famous dictum is in a sense embodied in the high proportion of space allocated to staff, including a dedicated back stair and live-in maids' rooms. The busier service rooms overlook the street; their fenestration is cleverly arranged to suggest a single contiguous window.

Free living

The open plan is the essential Modernist tenet. At No. 64, sliding screens allow the dining room, library and deeply bow-fronted drawing room, all of which face the garden, to be run together as a single space. The same often applied to children's rooms.

Neighbours

Two sets of architects built sympathetically paired but different houses for separate clients on adjacent sites carved from a single plot. Walter Gropius and Maxwell Fry's No. 66 has been significantly altered externally; the only change to No. 64 is a new conservatory.

High and over

Steel, often tubular, was used in Modernist buildings for handrails and balustrades. The emphasis was invariably horizontal. Low window sills created a greater connection with the outside. The concrete purity of such buildings can be an illusion – No. 64 is of white-rendered brick.

10 Palace Gate

Location *London SW8*
Date *1936–39*
Architect *Wells Coates*

Living room
The projecting annexe contains conventional, small flats, one per floor. A much narrower link or core holding the stair and two lifts (one for trade) connects this to the wide principal block. Open galleries are for deliveries and escape – the corridor is beyond it.

Modernism proved more popular in apartment blocks. Here, Coates deployed his ingenious 'three-two' section, based on his own flat nearby, although ultimately deriving from Russian sources. Along one side of the building, the ceiling of the bottom flat is raised while the floor of the top flat is dropped into the same space to meet it, resulting in each gaining a lofty, height-and-a-half living area. Along the other side, the middle storey is filled with other rooms and access corridors with steps up or down to the two flats.

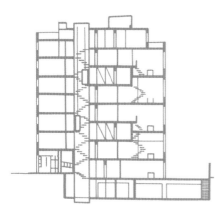

Split section

In the main block, three storeys toward the street – containing bathrooms, bedrooms and the access corridor – match just two toward the rear, allowing taller living areas overlooking the garden. Levels within flats are linked by simple stairs ('upper' flats) or a spiral staircase ('lower').

Both sides now

Each floor has bedrooms. One faces the street and two the garden but these are stacked, occupying the same height as the living room, and so the three-two concept is seen along the main block as well as across it.

Intricate plan

Flats are dual aspect, spanning the block. The living rooms have open fires. Kitchens have their own 'back' door, on the same level as the tenants', but accessed from the gallery. This is reached from the service lift, which starts in the basement.

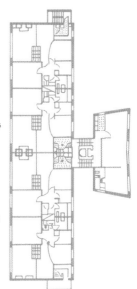

A view to improve

A wide sash window in the rear wall of the living room floods it with air and light. Coates, a qualified engineer, used an innovative concrete structure that meant rooms could be combined vertically or horizontally without prejudicing its integrity.

169

Location Map

With most of the building types we know today now fixed, the inter-war years were marked by their architectural evolution. Education, leisure, commerce and retail adopted the style that suited them best, from the sombre strength of the Senate House or the Underground's head office to the exciting, aerodynamic lines of the New Victoria Cinema, Broadcasting House or the Daily Express building.

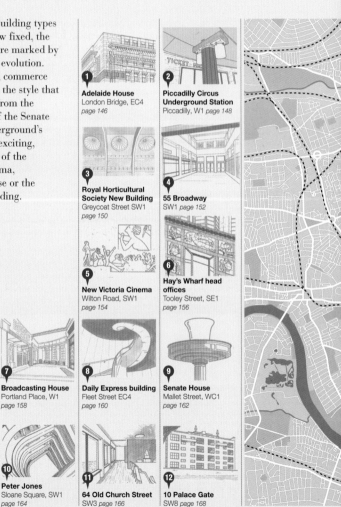

1 **Adelaide House**
London Bridge, EC4
page 146

2 **Piccadilly Circus Underground Station**
Piccadilly, W1 *page 148*

3 **Royal Horticultural Society New Building**
Greycoat Street SW1
page 150

4 **55 Broadway**
SW1 *page 152*

5 **New Victoria Cinema**
Wilton Road, SW1
page 154

6 **Hay's Wharf head offices**
Tooley Street, SE1
page 156

7 **Broadcasting House**
Portland Place, W1
page 158

8 **Daily Express building**
Fleet Street EC4
page 160

9 **Senate House**
Mallet Street, WC1
page 162

10 **Peter Jones**
Sloane Square, SW1
page 164

11 **64 Old Church Street**
SW3 *page 166*

12 **10 Palace Gate**
SW8 *page 168*

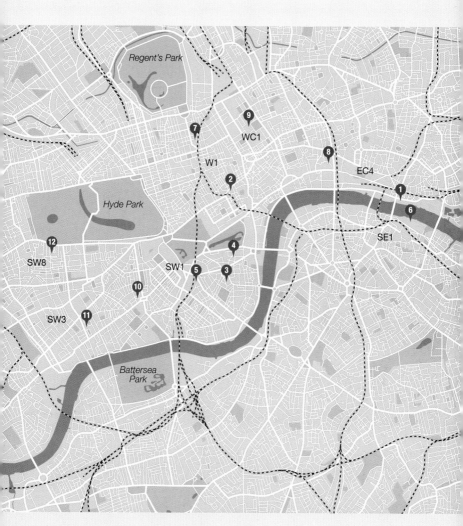

Regent's Park

9

7

WC1

W1

2

Hyde Park

8

EC4

1

6

SE1

12

4

SW8

5

3

SW1

10

SW3

11

Battersea
Park

Introduction

After 1945 there was renewed conviction that public architecture should have an avowedly social function, while private and institutional buildings struck out in new directions. Modernism remained but developed two further strands – the tougher New Brutalism, a label that soon lost one word and gained notoriety for

the other (which derives from *béton brut*, French for raw concrete), and the crisp, technologically inspired Corporate Modernism. The new discipline of town planning was an enabler, through comprehensive redevelopment, although London's ownership structure once again proved resistant beyond small pockets.

Concrete proposal
Post-war architecture is most often associated with the 'honest' use of concrete. The Alexandra and Ainsworth housing estate embodies this.

Churchill Gardens

Location
*Churchill Gardens Road
London SW1*

Date *1946–62*

Architects *Philip Powell
and Hidalgo Moya*

Evolving from the County of London Plan of 1943, which addressed both pre-war slum clearance and post-war reconstruction with Modernist doctrine, this council estate of over 1,600 homes in more than three dozen concrete-framed blocks was viewed as a model of urban residential development. Mixing 11-storey 'slab' blocks with lower maisonettes and terraces achieved the maximum permitted density without monotony, while shops, a library and extensive open space added to its appeal. It remains well regarded today, unlike many that followed.

Modern community
Variations in articulation and materials, partly brought about by phased construction, also soften the end result. Brick is used in the early stages, with projecting stair towers; frosted glass balconies, white glazed brick and *pilotis* (columns) came later. Colour provided accents throughout.

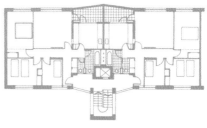

Sunshine state

The layout is considered. Slab blocks are orientated north-south for optimum exposure to sunlight according to the *Zeilenbau* principle, which originated in the 1920s at the progressive German Bauhaus design school. This also gave protection from road noise. Terraces parallel the river.

Light and airy

The flats were conventionally planned but dual-aspect. Angled open-air patios leading off the living rooms broaden into perimeter balconies in some blocks. Costs were reduced by arranging the kitchens – which also open onto the patios – as mirror-imaged pairs around the 'wet' services and lift.

Fitting in

Adventurous play areas for children were part of the amenities and the hard landscaping. This and the positioning and shape of the new roads were considered to break down the scale of the estate and stitch it into its surroundings.

Back to the future

In height, length, façade modulation and hue the final phase emulates the stuccoed Victorian terrace it faces. The estate was heated from the waste hot water of nearby Battersea Power Station, a polygonal glass tower acting as an accumulator or store.

Royal Festival Hall

Location
Belvedere Road
London SE1
Date *1948–51; 1963–64*
Architects *Robert Matthew, Leslie Martin, Peter Moro and others; Norman Engleback*

Changing places

Years later new cladding and fenestration, more rooms and foyers and ultimately – infamously – a concrete collar of elevated walkways joining it to other elements of the South Bank complex altered the building significantly. More recent changes reversed some of this.

This new concert hall, replacing the Blitzed Queen's Hall, was the architectural centrepiece of the main Festival of Britain site and the only building intended to be permanent. In shaking up the stuffiness of the type with a Modernist plan of free-flowing space, places to linger inside and out and even non-hierarchical bars, it also symbolised the less elitist and more democratic society that began to appear after the war. It was the first step in the transformation of an industrial district into a cultural destination.

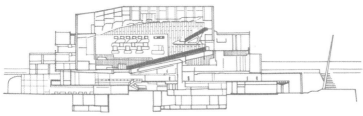

Suspended animation

The auditorium is an independent volume isolated from noise and vibration primarily by being raised above the ground floor. This also frees space beneath it, allowing people to circulate quickly and easily and connecting areas together. Entry is from ground and first floors.

'Egg in the box'

Martin's description is apt. Columns below and parts of the structure around it support the auditorium, a double skin of concrete further insulates and steel trusses permit a clear-span roof. The 'open drawer' boxes are angled for good sightlines. Controversy surrounded its recent refurbishment.

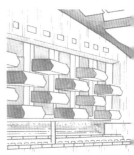

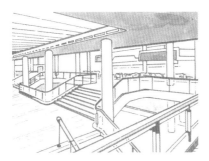

For the people

In the face of continued rationing, hardwoods, bronze, polished fossil limestone and bespoke fabrics gave a sense of luxury. The informality of access, physically and culturally, was reflected in sweeping, cantilevered staircases, asymmetric entrances and roof terraces.

Improved outlook

Only now do Le Corbusier's 'Five Points of a New Architecture', codified a generation ago, arrive publically: *pilotis*, the open plan, a façade divorced from its load-bearing role, strip or horizontal windows and the roof as a useable 'fifth façade'. Interiors bore Scandinavian influences.

Congress House

Congress House & Congress Centre

Location
Great Russell Street
London WC1

Date *1948–57*

Architect *David du Rieu*
Aberdeen

The Trades Union Congress commissioned this imaginatively planned building to serve as a new head office and memorial to its war efforts. Designed before but built after the Festival Hall, it is arguably a purer interpretation of Modernist principles. Behind differently treated façades three wings of offices, meeting rooms and the chairman's flat surround a courtyard, unusually the centre of the plan, with Jacob Epstein's commemorative sculptural group within it and the large hall beneath. Inverted, too, is the main stair, leading down rather than up.

Urbane presence

A rectilinear polished granite and strip-window façade floats above Great Russell Street on *pilotis*. The off-centre entrance is marked by Bernard Meadows's *The Spirit of Trade Unionism*. On the Dyott Street elevation, balconies are borrowed from Gropius's Bauhaus building in Dessau, Germany.

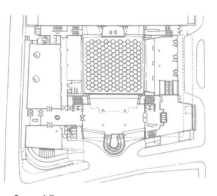

Ground floor

At the stair, rotating 90 degrees reveals the building's true axis. Ahead, across the glass-floored courtyard, Jacob Epstein's *Pieta* stands against mosaic (originally marble slabs) affixed to what is in essence the party wall with the next building; behind, one descends to the Memorial Hall.

Right angle

Further along Dyott Street curves appear: the projection covering an underground car-park ramp, the top storey set-backs and the deep, fully glazed half-drum that houses the horseshoe-shaped stair, the pivot on which the building – and the visitor – turns.

Pieta

Lost on a field of green and distanced by a sea of glass, a helmeted soldier lies dead in his mother's arms. Carved in situ from a 10-tonne block of stone, enclosed by towering walls, profound, this was Epstein's last work in stone.

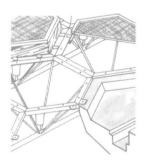

Floor and roof

The courtyard is formed of hexagonal glass blocks held in a steel space frame, allowing natural light into the hall below. Problems with water penetration led to overcladding with additional glazing, removed in 2016 after the entire courtyard was given a polymer roof.

45–46 Albemarle Street

Location *London W1*
Date *1955–57*
Architect *Ernö Goldfinger*

Mayfair's grid-like streets, with their uniform Georgian architecture and standard plots, presented challenges and opportunities alike for Modernists seeking to replace buildings lost in the war. Hungarian Goldfinger had already encountered difficulties when building a terrace of contemporary houses (including his own) in suburban Hampstead but was hired by Arnold Lee of Imry Properties, one of the new breed of commercial developers, to erect this concrete-framed infill block just off Piccadilly. It embodies a number of principles Goldfinger was to make his own.

Working space
A semi-detached composition, the building comprises a basement, two ground-floor retail units and five floors of offices. Though anticipated for vertically separated occupation about the centre line, floors could be (and have been) combined, storey by storey, via special dividing walls.

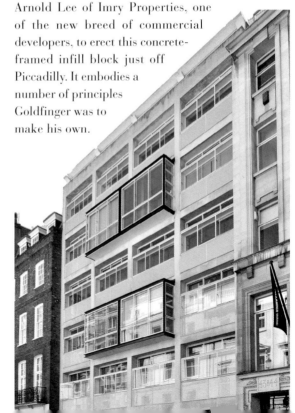

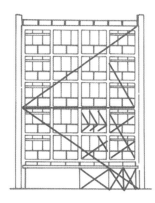

In proportion

As controlled as a Georgian house, the façade is set out using the Golden Section. A mathematical ratio known in antiquity and popularised in the 18th century, this was thought to produce visually pleasing relationships that echoed aspects of nature.

Recede, advance

Windows are set back at the top, creating a horizontal plane that bounces light inside, whereas fully glazed oriels project. Attached to the façade rather than being cantilevered from it on concrete beams, these are 'dishonest' according to some Modernist theorists.

Rearguard action

Goldfinger took as much care over the rear elevation, where toilet towers save space on the main floors. The basic fenestration is identical. Brick plus bush-hammered (power-tooled) and smooth concrete contrast with the Portland stone of the Albemarle Street front.

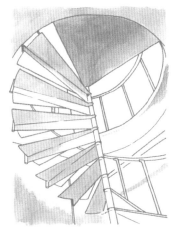

Space saver

As a speculative building, flexibility and convenience helped secure a let. A steel spiral staircase joins the ground floor to the basement and the finish was to 'shell and core' standard, where detailed fitting-out is left to tenants. Goldfinger designed parts of No. 46's himself.

Barbican

Location *Silk Street London EC2*
Date *1955–82*
Architects *Chamberlin, Powell & Bon*

The northern edge of the City of London was devastated in the Blitz. Residential reconstruction aimed to bring a substantial population back to the Square Mile, providing rentable homes for professionals and what today are called key workers – teachers, police and others. Building on their success with the Golden Lane estate immediately to the north, for which they had partnered, the young practice of Peter 'Joe' Chamberlin, Geoffrey Powell and Christoph Bon proposed an initial scheme that took another decade to start. As built, it has no equal.

Past, present, future
Predicated on the contemporary notion of separating vehicles and pedestrians vertically, the estate is a self-contained community. Resident-only lawns, water gardens and underground parking are complemented by retained remains of a Roman fort, whose rubble walls informed the Barbican's rough concrete finish.

High living

Three triangular towers, then the tallest in Europe, signal the estate from afar and form its architectural background. Three flats per floor have bedrooms and a corner living area opening onto a balcony along the façade. Service rooms are further inside and mostly windowless.

New inside

A generation comfortable with European food, travel and design found compact galley kitchens with waste disposal, lounges with full-height windows and a sliding door onto a terrace and electric underfloor heating. Supermarkets were still rare so hatches allowed regular deliveries of fresh produce.

Tradition and modernity

Georgian squares, crescents and mews are referenced in the horizontal terraces and other low blocks, but also novel pre-war theories for urban living by Le Corbusier. These homes are at street level, on (and beneath) the podium or Highwalk and on upper storeys.

Art for all

Cultural facilities were always intended but were added to by government diktat after construction had begun, leading to the majority being buried below ground. With great skill, an art gallery, library, theatre, cinemas and concert hall were eventually fitted in.

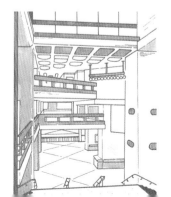

183

New Zealand House

Location *Haymarket London SW1*

Date *1956–63*

Architect *Robert Matthew*

The New Zealand High Commission was one of the first British examples of Corporate Modernism, an evolution of the International Style that combined a steel frame, sophisticated curtain walling and high-quality interiors and was created by European architects who had settled in the United States. Rapidly adopted by that country's industrial giants after the war, the style often featured a lower block or podium supporting a narrower tower, as with Lever House in New York, completed in 1952. The height and sensitive location of this London version caused arguments.

Diplomatic immunity
Design negotiations modified the height of the podium, which now matches the cornice line of its neighbours. A recessed terrace was for the high commissioner's use. New Zealand House was well specified; it was the first building of its type with full air-conditioning.

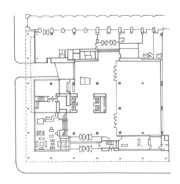

Plan

Further effort was made to integrate the building with its surroundings with shops complementing the adjacent Royal Opera Arcade by John Nash and a secondary entrance leading off from it. The double-height reception is one of several spaces that have since been modified.

Lobby

The ground floor is set back slightly behind stainless steel columns acting as *pilotis*. Fully glazed, it is penetrated by a canopy. These stratagems draw visitors in. Beyond the glass, more columns, a slatted hardwood ceiling and the cutaway mezzanine floor continue the effect.

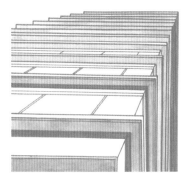

Greenhouse effect

Projecting floor slabs function aesthetically and practically, as cleaning ledges and vertigo mitigation. The air-conditioning worked in conjunction with blinds, some automatic, and part double glazing. The phenomenon of solar gain was not properly understood and replacement blinds must today be kept down.

Penthouse

A lounge is situated on the top floor. Panoramic views over central London can be obtained through full-height windows; these are also set back, permitting a further open-air terrace that continues around the tower's perimeter. The 'trellis' beams are common on period tower roofs.

Sanderson House

Sanderson

Location *Berners Street London W1*

Date *1957–60*

Architect *Reginald Uren (architect), Beverley Pick (interior design), Philip Hicks (landscape architect)*

Though Corporate Modernism soon came to symbolise power and progress, it was not confined to skyscrapers, even in its homeland. Its technocratic image suited companies relocating to suburban or greenfield sites, where the university-derived 'campus' model was used, and also made a bold declaration in urban environments. Completed for the centenary of wallpaper and textile makers Arthur Sanderson & Sons Ltd, this careful blend of low- and mid-rise buildings north of Oxford Street deploys the style. Much altered, it is now a hotel.

Calling card
The firm, which decorated the Festival Hall, made a clear statement with the building. It contained elaborate public showrooms to the south, divided by a courtyard from trade counters and design studios to the north. A car park and stockroom lay below ground.

Courtyard plan

Cars drove through the Berners Street frontage to the courtyard, formed by a taller tower and two minor wings behind the main range. Its Japanese-inspired planted water garden of slate, marble and stones is backed by an abstract coloured mosaic-veined mural by Jupp Dernbach-Mayen.

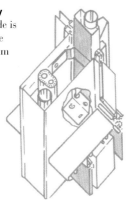

Service technology

The principal façade is proportioned by the expressed aluminium mullions at 1.4 m (4 ft 6 in) centres. They carry service runs for pipes inside and outside the glazing. Spandrels are opaque glass, coloured turquoise on the first floor and grey above.

Stained-glass screen

A vast backlit stained-glass panel by John Piper, who was also employed at the new Coventry Cathedral, greeted visitors. Featuring stylised plants in blocks of brilliant colour, it is thought to be his largest secular piece, at 9.8 m by 6.4 m (32 ft by 21 ft).

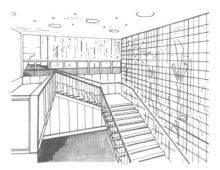

Space-age stair

The 'flying' customer stair has open timber treads and aluminium balustrading. It led originally to retail showrooms on the first, second and third floors, a series of room sets that changed seasonally. Day- and artificially lit, they included a double-height display space with mezzanine.

26 St James's Place

Location *London SW1*
Date *1959–60*
Architect *Denys Lasdun*

The 'three-two' split section used by Wells Coates at 10 Palace Gate (page 168) was adopted two decades later by Lasdun, who had worked with Coates, for this block of luxury, serviced apartments adjacent to Spencer House (page 54) and Bridgewater House (page 76). Once more, the height-and-a-half living rooms have the best view, here of Green Park, and once more, the principle is applied longitudinally as well as laterally. The articulation and materials palette, though, are representative of the new era.

Parking space
The disposition of split-level and single-storey apartments, these last on the middle floors of each group of three, is signalled by grey Baveno granite on short balconies and floor bands against blue engineering brick. Lasdun used similar contrasts to indicate functions on other projects.

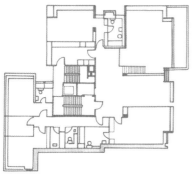

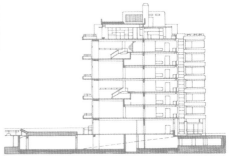

Plan

The large flats have five bedrooms and almost as many bathrooms (including an en suite). As at Palace Gate, the kitchen is entered directly from a separate service stair and lift. Structural walls are minimal, for flexibility, a common Lasdun principle.

Interior

An open-tread stair connects upper and lower levels. Construction techniques were improving in less visible ways, too: the flats were insulated thermally and acoustically with cork-lined walls and floors suspended on battens with fibreglass quilting, and each room had discrete thermostatically controlled convector heating.

Section

With one flat per floor there is no need for access corridors, freeing more space. Reinforced concrete balconies cantilevered 2.1 m (7 ft) from the façade introduce another concept that would become central to Lasdun's architecture, sometimes on a grand scale.

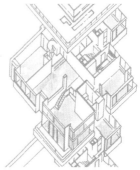

Three dimensions

An axonometric shows how the living area floor is lowered on the corner toward the park. This is matched by a raised ceiling in the flat below. Single-storey flats wrap around this intrusion and so are L-shaped. All three elevations are extensively glazed.

Royal College of Physicians

Location
*St Andrews Place
London NW1*
Date *1959–64*
Architect *Denys Lasdun*

With this remarkable building Lasdun placed an institution steeped in a level of tradition akin to that of an Oxbridge college or a livery company – including formal robing, processional ritual and oral examinations in a closed room – within an audaciously Modernist composition that was itself inserted into a Nash terrace looking out onto Regent's Park. Innovative in plan and section, the distinction between inside and outside is often blurred to take full advantage of the handsome setting. Both combine to generate imposing and intimate views alike.

Doctors' prescription
The west front enclosing the library and entrance hovers above the park on concrete stilts.
As with Lasdun's 26 St James's Place (page 188) materials define different usages: fixed, ceremonial spaces are clad in off-white mosaic, changeable, functional spaces in blue engineering brick.

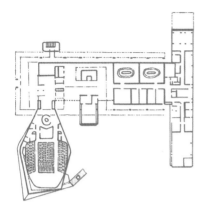

Ground floor

The plan arose from the site and Lasdun's painstaking observations of college life. A new terrace on Albany Street repairs Blitz damage, a wing for the principal rooms and a spur for the lecture theatre extend into the park. Note the projecting Censors Room.

Square stair

Placed at the heart of the ceremonial route, the free-standing stair expands with each turn until it reaches the first floor. With a narrower mezzanine above that, every level can be seen from every other. Amidst more mosaic are marble, stained glass and brass.

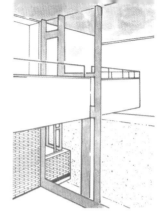

Invisible barrier

Lasdun uses many devices to break down the distinction between inside and outside. Slit windows suddenly reveal slices of the landscape, floor-to-ceiling plate glass embraces it in vistas and walkways push through walls to become exterior balconies.

Shaping up

Single-, double- and even triple-height volumes of varying form and size are encountered: the punctured box of the Censors Room, divisible rectangular dining hall and polygonal lecture theatre. Space flows and daylight penetrates, helped by absent corners and walls stopping short of ceilings.

Centre Point

Location
*New Oxford Street
London WC2*
Date *1959–66*
Architect *George Marsh
(architect), William
Frischmann (engineer)*

Few of London's buildings have proved so enduringly controversial as this slim 121 m (398 ft tower), one of the tallest of the new breed that resulted from improved engineering techniques. The deal between its developer and the planning authorities that allowed its great height, the lack of public awareness even as construction began and the lengthy period during which it remained empty all left their mark, yet the dynamic result remains one of the capital's most effective architectural declarations.

'The man who built London'
Marsh worked for Richard Seifert, whose ability to extract the maximum value from a given plot led to similar commissions across London such as Space House, Tolworth Tower and Croydon's NLA Tower. Each was distinctive but all conformed to a recognisable 'house' style.

Higher and higher

The subtly facetted concrete T-pieces that form the tower's façade are actually structural. They were pre-cast off-site and delivered in sequence. The top floors were intended for restaurant use and are surmounted by an open-air viewing deck and a cornice whose profile echoes the elevation.

Upper entrance

Originally the tower's ground floor was open, the entrance being a storey higher and reached by external staircases. The forecourt fountain pool was removed in conjunction with works for Crossrail. The building's name comes from its position at the junction of three post codes.

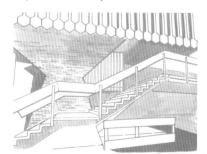

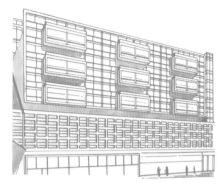

Hip homes

The tower, containing offices, was part of what today is known as a mixed-use scheme. A pub, bank, shops and more offices with maisonettes above were connected by a wide, two-storey link bridge of toughened plate glass. It sits upon Seifert's signature waisted *pilotis*.

Minimal art

The elevated reception displays abstract sculpted relief panels typical of the period; the black-and-white patterned floor was also used by Marsh in his home. The bank featured mosaic and sculptural work. The entire complex has now been remodelled as apartments.

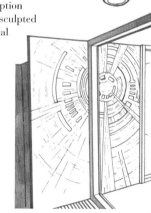

GPO Tower

BT Tower

Location *Maple Street London W1*

Date *1961–65*

Architects *Eric Bedford, George Reginald Yeats (architects), L.R. Creasy (engineer)*

The number of tall buildings springing up during the 'Swinging Sixties' threatened the General Post Office's telecommunications network – it relied on microwaves that are disrupted by anything blocking their path. To address the problem, especially during the ongoing Cold War, aerials and equipment at London's main exchange were lifted 190 m (625 ft) into the air on a new tower, taking them far above the height of any current or proposed development. This became not only the capital's but Britain's tallest building, a title it retained for more than 15 years.

Long-distance information
Still looking astonishingly modern today, the GPO Tower was the perfect embodiment of a technological decade that had already witnessed the laser, the hovercraft and the contraceptive pill, and would later welcome Concorde and the first moon landing.

Up and around

A thick reinforced concrete foundation raft supports a concrete pyramid that spreads the load of the tower. This is circular, to reduce wind resistance and ease aerial alignment. A 'collar' tied to the exchange provides bracing. A crane climbed with the tower.

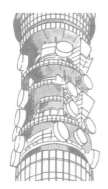

Glass, horn, dish

The stainless steel cladding has an opening inner pane, aluminium *brises soleil* ('sun breakers') and a green-tinted 'anti-sun' outer layer. The original horn aerials were replaced by dishes that have themselves now been superseded and removed: cranes are built in to the circumferential slot.

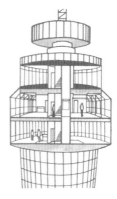

Cutaway

Served by two of the fastest lifts in Europe were three observation platforms (two open-air) and the famous revolving restaurant. Above it was the kitchen and cocktail bar. Public access to the tops of new television and radio towers was common across Europe.

Top of the world

The outer ring is 20 m (65 ft) in diameter and revolves once every 22 minutes, still driven by the original 1.5 kW (2 BHP) motor. The glazing moves with the ring for unobstructed views. The restaurant was closed to the public in 1980, nine years after a bomb explosion caused serious damage.

The Economist Group
The Economist Plaza

Location
*St James's Street
London SW1*

Date *1962–64*

Architects *Alison
Smithson, Peter
Smithson*

This scheme for *The Economist* business newspaper inserts towers and another post-war Modernist concept, the raised piazza, into the select district of Mayfair. That it succeeds is due to its compact size and the respect shown for the site. The New Brutalism practised by the Smithsons is expressive but disciplined, three towers – offices for the client, retail (principally a bank) and apartments for the public and Boodle's club, whose site it was – having differing heights, sizes and façade modules. Below are car parking, servicing and staff areas.

Street sober
Given its location, the group is appropriately unobtrusive from most angles. Along St James's Street, for example, the tallest tower is placed behind the four-storey bank, which itself continues the line of adjacent buildings. The spaces between the blocks aim to evoke Georgian streets.

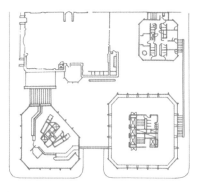

Gentle disposition

Elements address the whole differently. The residential block can be entered through Boodle's as well as from the street; the bank pavilion takes a prominent corner; the chamfered corner motif is repeated in miniature on the bay added to the club.

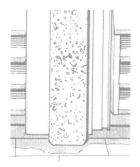

Material concerns

Expressive use of a given material need not imply honesty – tactility or visual appeal may be the primary motive. Here, slabs of fossil-rich Portland roach stone are spaced to show their application merely as decorative trim, while sheet aluminium conceals structural concrete.

Permeable piazza

Steps to the east and west and a ramp mediate between the varying street levels. Solid balustrading and a bench provide amenity. Two towers draw back from their footprint, leaving the strongly articulated structural columns to act as colonnades.

Open for business

Martin's Bank was entered on the diagonal. Escalators – a first for the company – led up to the double-height banking hall, which was day-lit through windows up to 14 sq m (150 sq ft) in size and had an illuminated ceiling. The space is now a restaurant.

National Theatre

Royal National Theatre

Location *Upper Ground London SE1*

Date *1962–76*

Architect *Denys Lasdun*

Layers

Three auditoria, based on stage configurations of the past (Greek amphitheatre, Tudor yard, Neoclassical proscenium arch), and all other spaces were formed from concrete, contentiously left exposed even indoors. A service road originally ran around the building, justifying the unloved elevated walkways.

When reconstruction plans for London were made during the war a site for a national theatre was identified on the South Bank, then an industrial area, as part of a major cultural centre. After years of delay and a shift of location downstream, adjacent to Waterloo Bridge, Lasdun was appointed. With lack of knowledge of the sector accounted an advantage, he worked closely with actors including Laurence Olivier to define a new kind of theatrical experience. The architecture, too, was novel for the type, its uncompromising Brutalism challenging convention.

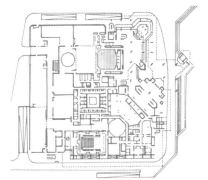

Strata (below)

Tumbling terraces, or strata as Lasdun termed them, linked the building to the riverside and bridge, encouraged people up from ground level to flow freely around the site and broke down its mass. The vertical fly towers and tall internal volumes counter this horizontality.

Direction

The theatre was planned from the inside out. Its main stage, lobby and barbed stair bastion lie on a principal axis which, at a 45 degree angle to the building façade, points meaningfully to the West End. Visibility from the bridge was also important.

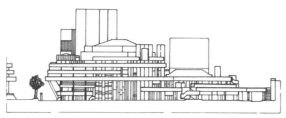

Space

The play of light, both natural and artificial, highlights a drama of voids and solids, bridges and overhangs. The 'egg-crate' coffering of the ceilings is purely structural – it saves weight – but enhances the effect. Interiors have been altered several times since completion.

Texture

When cast in situ, concrete is poured into wooden or metal moulds called shuttering or formwork. The National Theatre's alternated planks chosen for their strong grain and laid in contrasting directions with sanded lengths. All were planed to slightly different thicknesses.

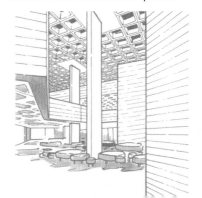

Lillington Gardens

Humane homes
This softer, more considerate architecture reflects the passage of time since the Modernist rigour of Churchill Gardens (page 174). Importantly, traditional materials like handmade, porous red-brown brick with raked mortar joints and small paviours replaced concrete, an approach known as contextual or vernacular architecture.

This public housing project for Westminster council stands out for the proof it provided that a usefully high density of dwellings could be fitted in to an urban environment without the need for either towers or long slabs, while also maintaining a sense of neighbourliness and a connection to the locale. Through ingenious planning, careful choice of materials and generous communal and private landscaping, mid-rise blocks were shown as sufficient to house 2,000 residents over three phases, with no block more than eight storeys high; the result was also attractive. This approach was somewhat influential.

Location
Vauxhall Bridge Road London SW1

Date *1961–74*

Architects *John Darbourne and Geoffrey Darke*

Facing change
In a further departure from the sometimes alienating uniformity of earlier Modernist housing, a wide diversity in plan and section directly drove the varied external appearance of the blocks. This increased feelings of familiarity and homeliness. Cars are also excluded, with parking underground.

Access some areas
Many flats are reached by stairs that pass alongside or even through blocks, to give individual front doors even on the higher levels. Galleries, walkways crossing voids and bridges are also encountered. The final phase's 'roof streets' developed the idea more fully.

Up and over
Internally, space was gained through split levels, as here, and the newly developed scissor section, where dual-aspect flats interlock vertically around an access corridor using half-storeys to manage changes of level; bedrooms occupy one side of the block, living rooms the other, reducing disruptive noise.

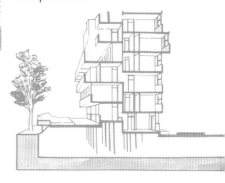

Roofscape
Density was achieved through complexity. Flats, studios, maisonettes and bedsits were mixed together and stacked, their varied shapes allowing balconies and other private spaces. Terraces, gardens, courts and planted areas were placed on upper levels and roofs. This also fragmented the massing.

Institute of Education, Clore Institute of Advanced Legal Studies

Spine...
Lasdun set a long, glass-clad spine on Bedford Way, partly to protect the University precinct behind but also to reinstate the line of a lost Georgian terrace – its set-backs match the cornices of the remaining houses.

Charles Holden's aborted masterplan for the University of London (page 162) was revisited in peacetime by Leslie Martin, who proposed a single, continuous block on a new north-south route along Bedford Way and the west side of Tavistock Square. The emerging conservation movement curtailed this in turn, but a reduced scheme by Lasdun to serve multiple institutions was approved. Both are examples of the megastructure, another post-war Modernist – indeed, Brutalist – vision whereby a colossal, monolithic building houses numerous, changeable functions within its flexible interior.

Location *Bedford Way, London WC1*
Date *1965–76*
Architect *Denys Lasdun*

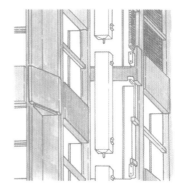

... and spur

To the west, short projecting wings were intended to contain teaching rooms, support spaces and lecture theatres in tiers that spill out to meet the pedestrianised plaza below. Abutted by aggressively modelled concrete escape stairs and topped by service core towers, only one was built.

Descent

A split-level lobby is entered from the street and the precinct, beneath which lies the lecture hall. A staircase winds around immense structural columns down a deep well to reach it. As at the National Theatre (page 198), the concrete was left uncovered.

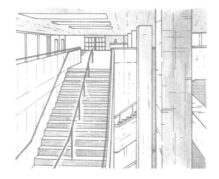

Glazing

The reinforced concrete structure is a hybrid. Poured-in-situ columns and beams support pre-cast load-bearing mullions. To these are attached prefabricated, bronze-anodised aluminium panels that carry the glazing. Lasdun continued this move away from bare concrete in his later works.

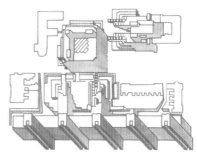

Unfinished business

Lasdun returned after completion to give each of the main occupiers a separate entrance and build the square library for the School of Oriental and African Studies. The third block, mirroring its longer brother, was intended for the Courtauld Institute but remained unbuilt.

Alexandra & Ainsworth Estate

Location *Rowley Way London NW8*

Date *1968–79*

Architect *Neave Brown (under Sydney Cook, borough architect)*

The newly formed borough of Camden quickly made a name for itself as the most progressive and ambitious provider of public housing in London. Determining that neither towers nor off-the-shelf 'system building' solutions were appropriate for urban accommodation, Cook chose this unpromising site alongside a mainline rail route for one of the most radical schemes of its time. Two parallel rows of four-storey buildings with a broad, green park between them are themselves sheltered by a taller block that curves alongside the railway for 425 m (1,400 ft).

My megastructure
Application of the megastructure purely to housing was unusual, although Le Corbusier envisaged a sinuous, 14 km (9 mile)-long coastal viaduct with apartments below it for Algiers. Though not planned for here, one perceived virtue of the megastructure was its potential for extension.

Cutting through

At each level, particularly in the principal block, the patio for one home is the roof of the one below. Shared external stairs link the maisonettes and houses. The park, with its multilevelled soft and hard landscaping, contains compartmented play areas.

Rooms with views (right)

Brown's reinterpretation of the terrace brought density, defensible space and sociability. Two-floor maisonettes are stacked; each has bedrooms on the lower level with living rooms above. These overlook the central pathway and have sliding doors to the balconies.

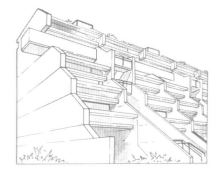

Stadium section

Borrowed from and named after its use in sports arenas, this reversal of the ziggurat deflected noise from the railway behind the block and, at the front, allowed for balconies on every level that were not over-sailed by the floor above.

Space station

The interiors are cleverly planned to make the most of the space available. Sliding panels can be used to divide the living room from the eat-in kitchen, whose built-in tiled work surface is an architectural feature. Behind the short, low wall are the stairs.

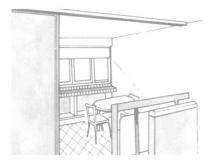

Location Map

London's rebirth after a cataclysmic war was gradual but, in parts, total. The large housing schemes – Churchill Gardens, the Barbican, Lillington Gardens and Alexandra and Ainsworth – span this period and the city, emulating in their scope the great estates of the past. Genuinely tall buildings, now impossible to ignore, begin their domination, with the new GPO Tower and Centre Point arguably the most and least loved, respectively.

❶ Churchill Gardens
Churchill Gardens Road, SW1 *page 174*

❷ Royal Festival Hall
Belvedere Road, SE1 *page 176*

❸ Congress House
Great Russell Street, WC1 *page 178*

❹ 45–46 Albemarle Street
W1 *page 180*

❺ Barbican
Silk Street, EC2 *page 182*

❻ New Zealand House
Haymarket, SW1 *page 184*

❼ Sanderson House
Berners Street, W1 *page 186*

❽ 26 St James's Place
W1 *page 188*

❾ Royal College of Physicians
St Andrews Place, NW1 *page 190*

❿ Centre Point
New Oxford Street, WC2 *page 192*

⓫ GPO Tower
Maple Street, W1 *page 194*

⓬ The Economist Group
St James's Street, SW1 *page 196*

⓭ National Theatre
Upper Ground, SE1 *page 198*

⓮ Lillington Gardens
Vauxhall Bridge Road, SW1 *page 200*

⓯ Institute of Education
Bedford Way, WC1 *page 202*

⓰ Alexandra & Ainsworth Estate
Rowley Way, NW8 *page 204*

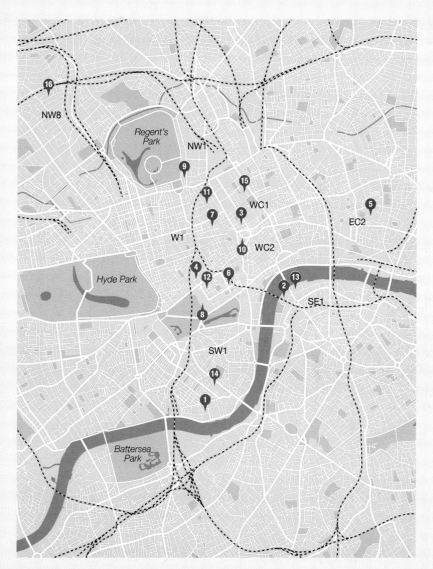

Introduction

Profound societal changes and successive energy crises saw the certainty of Modernism begin to evaporate. High Tech fetishised engineering over surface, Post-modernism's knowing, sometimes ironic take on Classicism, introduced humour and sustainability took root. The fragmented experiments of Deconstructivism, derived from philosophical theory, were genuinely

astonishing, while far more powerful and affordable computers released ideas previously confined to the drawing board through parametric visualisation and innovative structural calculation. A plurality of styles now greeted the new millennium, informing the London 2012 Olympics and the capital of today yet holding few clues as to tomorrow.

Brave new world
The towers of Canary Wharf stand for much more than trends in commercial architecture of the past four decades.

Lloyd's of London

Location *Lime Street London EC3*

Date *1978–86*

Architects *Richard Rogers Partnership (architects)*, *Peter Rice (engineer)*

This centuries-old insurance market had outgrown two purpose-built homes in 50 years. Turning to the joint architect of Paris's Pompidou Centre for a long-term solution was daring but inspired. Promising a strategy rather than a building, Rogers's analysis proved that conducting business face-to-face – a central principle of Lloyd's – could work by extending the critical underwriters' room (known as 'the Room') vertically, as an atrium, with escalators linking as many floors around it as were needed. An ingeniously engineered, finely finished reinforced concrete frame and externalised servicing maximised space. Very publicly, the new movement of High Tech had arrived.

Risky business
Many factors drove the building's controversial appearance. The externally braced, barrel-vaulted atrium roof recalls the Victorian Crystal Palace; the service towers, initially slender, had to be greatly enlarged at a late stage to accommodate additional computer cooling equipment. Their cranes are for maintenance.

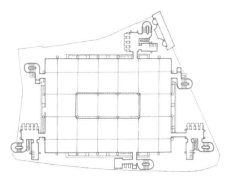

Square peg, round hole

Columns outline the atrium and define the building envelope, leaving unobstructed floorplates. Inserting this efficient rectangle into a typically irregular City plot left spaces for the towers. The larger three contain glass wall-climbing lifts, toilets (prefabricated) and ducting, the others principally emergency staircases.

Inside outside (below)

Placing the services – air-conditioning, water, heating, power – on the exterior, and in stainless steel, was also intended to ease maintenance. Components are logically grouped and their repetition suggests a machine. It also brings visual depth to the building, each face of which differs.

The Room

Glass balustrades denote those storeys that constitute the Room; others, with full-height glazing, are let to tenants. This apportionment can be changed as the market expands or contracts. Floors are supported by a three-part, pre-cast concrete bracket assembly attaching them to the columns.

Complex cladding

Extracted air passes between the triple-glazed panes of the windows, helping to reduce solar gain in summer and heat loss in winter. It is then removed via the 'fish tail' scoops and sent for processing. Rollers dimpled the glass to impart a sparkle.

211

British Library

Location *Euston Road London NW1*
Date *1978–97*
Architect *Colin St John Wilson*

Open book

Pressure of space forced the legal deposit function to be detached from the British Museum at Bloomsbury (page 64) in favour of the abandoned St Pancras station's goods yard. The set-back piazza, roofline and materials of the new building were conditioned by planners.

Before the Millennium Dome (page 224) took its place, this was the building Britain loved to hate – it was late, over budget, had insufficient room for its millions of volumes and was in any event surely redundant as the digital age dawned. However, the largest building erected in a century soon came to be appreciated for its exceptional craftsmanship, ample public space and intellectual content, and while its compromised nature has caused problems it remains the country's greatest contemporary civic enterprise. And books are still being printed.

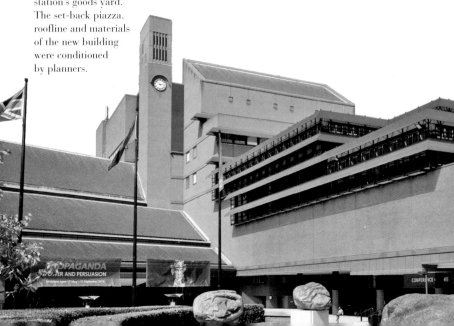

On the shelf

After repeated government vacillation, staccato staging and funding cuts, only about a third of this, the original design, was built. Preserved, though, was the split between reading rooms, with humanities to the west and sciences to the east. Four basement floors hold the books.

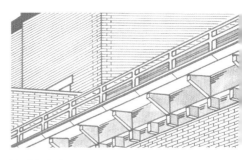

Dust jacket

The bricks are those used at the adjacent Midland Grand Hotel (page 90). Overall, the building essays a more romantic Modernism, an English equivalent to Alvar Aalto, Willem Dudok (whose Hilversum Town Hall is acknowledged in its tower) and Frank Lloyd Wright.

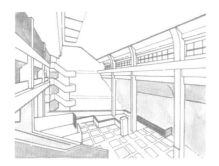

Foreword

The light-filled entrance hall, its paving inverting the pattern of the piazza, rises in waves toward the King George III book tower, installed – after genuine technological supersession – in place of the printed index. Tactile travertine, plaster, stone, leather and brass are the main materials.

Chapters

Disciplinary differences – science journals are consulted in multiples for short periods, humanities texts studied singly and at length – shaped the reading rooms and their bespoke desks and lighting. The building's structural column grid, not always apparent because of the vast scale, is clear here.

Broadgate & Finsbury Avenue

Archetype

Now universal, the mid-rise block containing deep-plan offices with the fewest possible columns overlooking a central atrium was new. Setting several around landscaped public space referencing London's squares but including artworks, shops, bars and leisure facilities attracted a new class of tenant.

This urban office campus on the site of Broad Street railway station and goods yard redefined commercial architecture in Britain, let alone London. Stuart Lipton imported American concepts for steel-framed, highly serviced and flexible space erected by fast-track construction under innovative management contracts. The minimalist, British-designed Finsbury Avenue predated (though partly anticipated) the ubiquitous information technology of the 1986 'Big Bang' stock market trading reforms, but the later, more muscular Broadgate, largely by the Chicago firm of SOM, epitomises that era.

Location *Liverpool Street, London EC3*
Date *1981–2015*
Architects *Arup Associates, Skidmore, Owings & Merrill, Foster + Partners, MAKE*

Empire building

Starting with the L-shaped Finsbury Avenue to the west, the estate has grown remorselessly, sitting over the tracks into Liverpool Street station in parts and even replacing buildings only 15 years old. There was no Roman Broad Gate – the name is a marketing invention.

Tricky tower

The latest extension of Broadgate comprises a paired tower and lower block. Built on foundations intended for a much shorter building, a five-storey-high steel A-frame diverts part of the former's weight onto more of the original piles and forms a dramatic open-air galleria.

Cutting edge

Arup's Finsbury Avenue used repetitive, prefabricated steel elements with simple, bolted connections. Structural atrium glazing allowed smaller-section pieces for a lighter effect. Water circulated through mullions and external shades of bronze-anodised aluminium were also maintenance gangways. Computerised trading floors were inserted easily when needed.

Bigger, bolder

Arup's first Broadgate blocks employed expanses of green-tinted glazing, giving glimpses of their atriums in High Tech fashion, followed by heavily articulated stone screens. SOM's buildings are very different; larger and brasher, their Postmodernist façades echo previous architectural styles in polished, coloured concrete and granite.

Cascades

Storm warning
Packed with colourful references to its location – the sloping profile recollects ships' sails, the blue engineering brick of the lower levels can be read as water – and outrageously high for the time, the wilfulness and even excess of Cascades was absolutely of its day.

In its early years, the Dockland redevelopment boom was also just a bubble. With little real idea of the potential for this truly enormous area – it sits as far to the east of Tower Bridge as White City does to the west – and a lack of connection to the rest of the city, the first forays were tentative. They did, though, coincide exactly with the rise of Postmodernism, and CZWG, the firm whose wit and irreverence put the 'arch' into architecture, built several of Dockland's signature initial schemes.

Location *Westferry Road, London E14*
Date *1985–88*
Architect *CZWG*

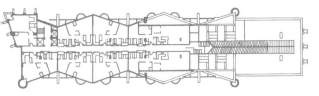

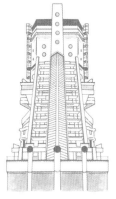

Ship shape

The concertina-like plan gives broad views from inside the apartments – across the entire Isle of Dogs, before Canary Wharf (page 222), for those facing east – and imitates the ripple of water. Amusingly, the fire escape ended near a swimming pool.

Sailor's hornpipe

The terraces and conservatories of the penthouses form the spine, the covered fire escape stair running between them. The stepped arrangement gives the development its name. The top band of darker brick and trio of vents or funnels evoke a ship's deck.

Crow's nest

Most flats have a balcony, of half- or three-quarter-circle plan. The resemblance to a crow's nest is inescapable, and indeed the tallest structure on the Isle of Dogs was once the Mast House, a tall enclosed crane for installing ships' masts. Cascades took its place, though was quickly overtaken.

Cabin fever

Porthole windows drive home the allusive conceit. These are formed of pre-cast concrete; the window pane turns on a central pivot. CZWG had earlier designed a jokey, *trompe l'oeil* interior for the home of critic Charles Jencks, whose 1977 book popularised the term 'Postmodernism'.

National Gallery Sainsbury Wing

Location
*Trafalgar Square
London WC2*
Date *1985–91*
Architects *Venturi,
Rauch & Scott-Brown
with Sheppard Robson
Architects*

Playing homage
Matching the material
and cornice line of the
original building, the
Sainsbury Wing also
appears to continue its
portico's Corinthian
colonnade. As with
much of this project,
however, not to mention
Postmodern architecture
in general, this is
something of an illusion.

This controversial extension to the Victorian gallery began with a competition to design a major new wing on a long-vacant site to the west. It proved inconclusive, not least due to the tensions created by a government stipulation that commercial office space be included to fund the building, and yielded only the unbuilt scheme infamously derided as a carbuncle by the Prince of Wales. When the Sainsbury brothers' philanthropy finally permitted a purely curatorial programme, the practice of Robert Venturi, a key Postmodernist figure, was ultimately selected.

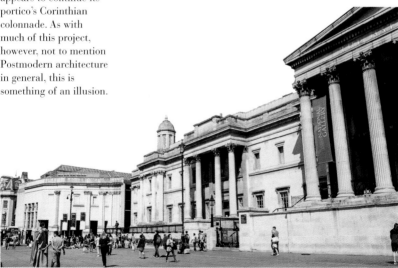

Fading façade

As the Wing moves away from the main building its pilasters, initially clustered, spread out and die away. Above them the entablature diminishes in detail, balustrade solidifying and dentils (small blocks) disappearing, and between, blind window reveals become shallower and shallower before vanishing altogether.

Renaissance stair

Appropriately, considering the Wing houses the Italian Renaissance collection, the grand staircase resembles those in Venetian *palazzos* (though hugely enlarged): in fact it was modelled after the Vatican's 17th-century Scala Regia. Both are constructed in forced perspective to seem longer than they actually are.

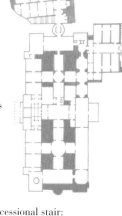

Enfilade plan

The Wing continues the long axis of the Gallery's *piano nobile* level, cleverly given the orientation of the new rooms. A sheer wall of smoked glass flanks the processional stair; stylistically the gap between old and new, signalled by the drum, is a chasm.

Italian job

Tuscan columns made of the same Italian stone used throughout the interior support round-arched gallery thresholds along the axis. Other rooms have square-headed openings. The whole, with places to sit and watch the activity, conjures the feel of an Italian hill town.

No. 1 Poultry

Location *London EC2*
Date *1986–98*
Architects *James Stirling, Michael Wilford and Associates*

Forty years of argument stand behind this building. When a plan by the site owner to replace its listed Victorian buildings with a glass skyscraper by Mies van der Rohe was refused, a second and very different concept was launched by his son. Two public inquiries and a hearing before the highest court in the land eventually enabled demolition of the existing buildings, closure of a network of small streets and the new block's erection, although by then the architect had died. The completed building remains controversial.

Out of time

Executed posthumously by Wilford. Stirling's vividly striped Postmodernist form in red and buff sandstone includes shops and an entrance to Bank underground station behind the colonnades, and a pedestrian way across the site. Designed in 1988, it was not built until ten years later.

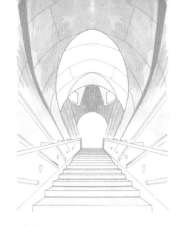

Worm's-eye view

This very individual projection technique was used extensively in Stirling's practice. Here it shows the street level and basement public areas – the entrance to the office floors at the apex, the open-air passageway through the building and the escalators to the Tube below.

Stairway to heaven

Originally intended as the main route to the offices, a theatrical staircase is concealed behind the ground-floor apex entrance. Entirely enclosed by a vaulted roof and with steps emerging from a constantly sloping floor, small windows provide natural light.

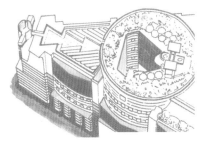

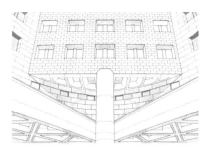

Rooftop restaurant

Conversely, an aerial view reveals the popular amenity on top of the building. Even this feature manifests the importance of geometry to the overall architecture, which is also evident in the hexagonal courtyard, the drum in which it sits and the façade bays.

Courtyard

Intersecting solids and voids, found throughout Stirling's work, are seen where the office floors engage the drum that straddles the public passageway, indicated by the triangular ceiling coffers and segmented fillets. The drum is open to the sky above and undercroft below.

Canary Wharf

Location
West India Avenue
London E14

Date *1985–*

Architects *Skidmore,
Owings & Merrill
(masterplan and
architects), César Pelli &
Associates, Foster +
Partners and others
(architects)*

'Wall Street on water'
The consortium of
finance houses planned
as tenants of this
audacious scheme fell
through, but rescue by
an agile Canadian
property firm finally
ensured the start of
construction in 1988.
More than 100,000
workers and 1.3 million
sq m (14 million sq ft)
later, its growth
continues.

Representing the single biggest change to London's
built environment since the war and also, post Big
Bang, a perceived threat to the Square Mile's pre-
eminence as its financial heart, the Canary Wharf
development transformed acres of derelict quays and
warehouses over a generation. The genesis was a
conversation between an American banker and French
restaurateur about siting a foodpacking operation and
the banker's realisation that his support office might
usefully be accommodated, too. After his property
advisor envisioned their entire concern moving, along
with their competitors, history had been made.

Special relationship

Unlike the contemporaneous Broadgate (page 214), which emulated London squares in its layout, Canary Wharf – with far more land available, nominal planning constraints and a more internationalised outlook – utilised a grander, axial, Beaux-Arts grid as its framework.

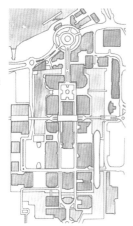

Prefab history

The lower blocks around the tower were deliberately designed in a variety of styles to simulate agedness. Thus the 'bricks' of SOM's Chicago School-like 10 Cabot Square are prefabricated panels, the 'stone' is concrete and its columns are made of fibreglass-reinforced cement.

Fast glass

Newer buildings on the estate are undemonstrative and minimalist, with unitised all-glass cladding units – combining window, insulation and all related fittings – clipped to steel frames and poured concrete floors. Such a system has also meant old but sound structures can be reclad and updated.

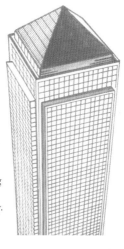

High water mark

Centrepiece of phase one was Pelli's One Canada Square, Britain's new tallest building, built – like much of the Wharf – over water. Stainless steel acts as a rainscreen, protecting the structural walls and reflecting the sky. It can be cleaned automatically.

Millennium Dome
The O$_2$ Arena

Time machine

Inspired by the brief and the personal interests of architect partner in charge Mike Davies, the Dome has 12 masts (for the months of the year, the hours and the 12 constellations that help measure time) and is 365 m (1,198 ft) across, matching the days in the year.

Criticism of the 'Millennium Experience' – marking the turn of the 21st century – that was planted on the then-remote Greenwich Peninsular has obscured the qualities of the building it was housed within. The reputation of Rogers and other High Tech architects was founded on their interest in lightweight, changeable structures using dry, precision-made components from the aviation and marine industries. The Dome's steel masts, cables and Teflon skin are therefore a logical progression from these beginnings, making an impressive yet accessible shelter for a million square feet of infinite possibility.

Location *Peninsular Square, London SE10*

Date *1996–99*

Architects *Richard Rogers Partnership (architects), Buro Happold Consulting Engineers (engineers)*

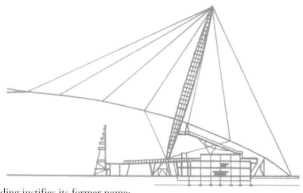

Raising the roof

Only the shape of the building justifies its former name: domes are self-supporting, through compressive strength, whereas this is in reality a tented enclosure held up by a catenary suspended from masts. These are in turn secured to anchor points around the circumference.

Highly strung

The covering, of Teflon-coated fibreglass, is attached to two cable nets. One is radial, the lines converging at the very centre, the other concentric. These connect by more cables to the tops and bottoms of the masts. A tension membrane results.

Support act

Each mast is fabricated from steel tubing, is nearly 91 m (300 ft) tall and sits on four 9 m (30 ft)-long legs, splayed to absorb movement. Circular, cage-like service units next to each one held air-conditioning, power and fire-fighting water tanks.

Inside job

The covering is translucent for good light levels, and the mast legs barely intrude into the floorspace. In 2007, as part of the long-promised wider development of the locale, the Dome was converted into a live event arena and other entertainment venues.

30 St Mary Axe

Location *London EC3*
Date *1997–2004*
Architects *Foster + Partners*

After a fatal bomb attack devastated the Edwardian Baltic Exchange, new owners commissioned Norman Foster to plan the fourth-tallest building in the world for the site. Nicknamed the Erotic Gherkin, it was abandoned after protests. Reinsurer Swiss Re then purchased the plot for their head office, retaining the architect for a wholly different design. The result introduced a new generation of non-orthogonal or curvilinear towers, used half the energy of its conventional equivalent and gave the City and the capital a new, internationally recognised landmark. The (unwanted) nickname stuck.

New arrival
The circular plan and tapered form equalise daylight, views and air (the windows open) and help reduce buffeting at piazza level. Not, strictly speaking, parametric, the diagrid frame and cladding nevertheless benefited from iterative digital modelling to confirm their final profiles.

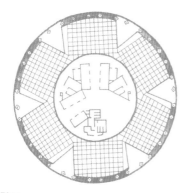

Plan

The positions of the wedge-shaped cut-outs rotate by 5 degrees on each successive storey, forming a series of gently twisting atriums crucial to the building's natural ventilation and generating the spirals of darker glass on its exterior. A solid firebreak is inserted every six floors.

Geometric glazing

Steel structural members produce column-free space within. Once the structure is clad, triangular, double-glazed window panels are attached. Flat and identical to ease manufacture and installation, they are backed by a large, active air gap with blinds that cools an internal glass skin beyond.

Advancing atriums

Daylight penetration is maximised by glass balustrades. Combined with the building's aerodynamic envelope and the opening windows, the atriums move air through the office floors albeit under a governed system. Gardens were originally intended for the balcony areas.

Summit

Usually devoted to plant, a glazed dome here permits a staggering hemispherical view from the communal bar. The crowning lens is the only curved piece of glass in the building. A restaurant occupies the floors below, with much of the displaced plant below that.

Peckham Library

Location
Peckham Hill Street
London SE15
Date *1998–99*
Architects *Alsop &*
Störmer

This new library and community facility in an inner-city location was one of the first major buildings in London to take a more challenging form, with its projecting upper levels. The strong colours and unusual textures of its metal mesh and patinated copper cladding were controversial. Much was due to the ethos of its lead designer, Will Alsop, but the client was pursuing a campaign of regeneration and therefore receptive to the possibilities for continuing a sequence of similarly-motivated projects around a new public square.

Urban intervention
The library was also unusual in having sustainability in mind. It was to be heated, cooled and ventilated through orientation and massing (the overhang protects the lower floors) with minimal mechanical assistance, although full air-conditioning has now been fitted.

228

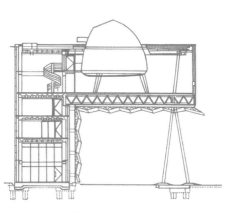

Cross-section

The main library is raised to the fourth and fifth floors, for the views (Alsop wanted users to appreciate their neighbourhood's position in the wider London landscape) and noise reduction. Architecturally startling, the structure remains conventional with steel and concrete columns and beams.

Bright and light

The double-height upper level is framed by reinforced concrete, cross-braced in places where wide panes of glass are fitted. The pods are reached from the fifth floor mezzanine, a spiral stair giving direct access to one for children from their dedicated library below.

Heart of glass

The rear elevation is entirely glazed, with contiguous panes in bold colours – including yellow, red and green – used to delineate rectilinear patterns. Some are in the shape of the library, while others follow areas of movement within it such as the staircases.

Pedagogic pods

Hoisted on tripods, the three curvaceous bulbs or pods originally also contained a meeting room and, in the open-topped example, a special collection. They are sheathed in extremely thin sheets of plywood. The library's raking steel supports continue through the floor to the roof.

Southwark Underground Station

Location
*Blackfriars Road
London SE1*

Date *1999*

Architects *MJP
Architects (architects),
Alexander Beleschenko
(artist), YRM/Anthony
Hunt (engineers)*

The Jubilee Line Extension added 11 stations to a line opened in 1979 but named after Queen Elizabeth II's Silver Jubilee two years earlier. Their architecture and engineering were intimately associated because of the difficulties of tunnelling under a congested city and finding suitable sites. Each was assigned to a different practice for diversity, although a unified materials palette was used on some elements. All were under the supervision of chief architect Roland Paoletti, who determined that stations should be brighter and less meanly dimensioned than was traditional.

Corner stone

The main entrance occupies a street corner, like many urban stations, but its curving form is reminiscent of those built for the Tube's suburban expansions between the wars. This introduces a theme that is repeated inside with many stylistic nods to those buildings.

Engineering ingenuity

The platforms lie under a Victorian railway viaduct serving nearby Waterloo East mainline station (to which Southwark is linked);

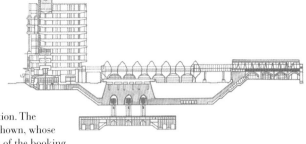

this complicated construction. The overstation development shown, whose rooftop drum mirrors that of the booking hall, has yet to materialise.

Concours d'Elégance

Paoletti's wish for daylight to reach as deeply into stations as possible is realised in the main concourse – though 15 m (50 ft) below the surface, a crescent-shaped rooflight allows light to penetrate and interact with a wall of 630 blue glass pieces.

Full circle (above)

The circular, double-height ticket hall remembers Charles Holden's work at Arnos Grove and Southgate on the Piccadilly Line. The small lantern light with its glass bricks and single column pays tribute to inter-war Underground architecture more generally.

Glass fin (right)

The opaque glass 'beacons' at the end of the short sets of stairs leading from the foot of the escalators to the platforms quote similar designs at Turnpike Lane station, opened in 1932. They also neatly and politely divide potentially conflicting streams of passengers.

The Shard

Location
London Bridge Street
London SE1

Date *2000–13*

Architects *Renzo Piano*
Building Workshop with
Adamson Associates
(architects), WSP
(engineers)

Sky line
Piano's inspirations for
the tower – originally
sketched over a meal
– have been cited as the
capital's historic church
steeples, the masts of
sailing boats that once
plied the Thames and
the railway lines of
the station it sits over.

The idea for what became the tallest building in the
European Union originated with developer Irvine
Sellar, who envisaged a vertical city of offices, a hotel,
places to dine and flats in a single building above the
London Bridge transport hub. Architect Renzo
Piano's response was radical – an elongated
pyramid over 300 m (1,000 ft) tall whose
glass façades converged in a tip that would
disappear. Surviving the financial crisis of
2008, the 72 floors of the London Bridge
Tower acquired a nickname (The Shard)
that was soon adopted as official.

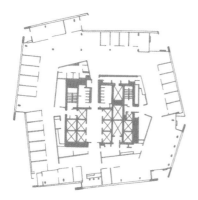

Changeable plan

The tapering form of The Shard fits its many functions. The lower, and so larger, floors suit open-plan offices, as seen here, whereas the higher, narrower storeys allow apartments to be dual-aspect. The hotel fits between the two. As such the building's floor plans differ throughout.

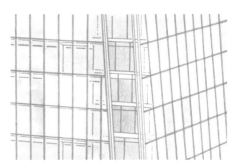

Lightness and solidity

Three layers of glass with a low iron content for extra clarity, a ventilated air gap and computerised blinds help environmental control, along with similarly arranged office winter gardens. The Shard was built upwards and downwards simultaneously. The concrete basement took 36 hours to pour.

Change of key

A structure that varies from steel to concrete and then back to steel as the building rises enables efficient office areas like this, the maximum number of hotel floors, its double-height lobby and a filigree observation deck. Hidden verticals increase floorspace.

Spire

Though inherent to Piano's concept, innovative tower summits were preferred by planners at the time to reduce monotony. The viewing gallery, partly open-air, is reached by the same double-deck lift as the restaurants. The hotel's heavy concrete frame also reduces building sway.

Maggie's West London

Location
Charing Cross Hospital
Fulham Palace Road
London W6

Date *2001–08*

Architects *Rogers Stirk*
Harbour + Partners
(architects), Dan
Pearson Studio
(landscape architect)

This is the first of the charitable network of cancer care day centres founded by Maggie Keswick Jencks, wife of the architectural critic Charles, to be built in England. Placed near but firmly separated from hospitals, they aim to provide a far more peaceful and comforting place to obtain support and advice, as well as somewhere just to talk. Their small scale and low cost has not deterred many well-known architects from contributing a design, including Frank Gehry and Zaha Hadid.

Restful refuge

Placed at the very corner of the hospital grounds and approached from them, Pearson's refreshingly clear landscaping forms a buffer.

A square spiral of hot orange wall, casual yet controlled, protects but doesn't corral the light spaces inside, aiding a feeling of openness.

Pavilion

The simple structure of the Centre revolves around a reinforced concrete portal frame that holds the 'floating' butterfly roof clear of the enfolding wall. Columns support the upper floors of the four separate enclosures within; clerestory window strips bring more daylight and glimpsed views.

Liminal place

Softening further the transition from the harsh environment of the hospital to the calming oases of the Centre, the planting continues in small patches and longer strips inside the wall. Large apertures, broad and low enough to sit on, do the same job.

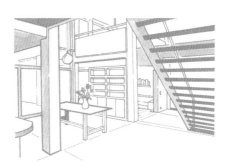

Framed

The open form of the building, with its unoppressive roof, coupled with the extensive glazing and landscaping promotes contact while catering for privacy. Courtyards, glass doors, gaps and natural ventilation make for an open and relaxing atmosphere.

Home from home

The cosy, domestic feel of the Centre is in complete contrast to the interior of the institutional building outside. The rooms, flexible enough for meetings, classes and talks, have sliding partitions and surround a double-height kitchen. There is no reception counter and no signage.

Graduate Centre, London Metropolitan University

Location
*Holloway Road
London N7*
Date *2003–04*
Architect *Studio
Libeskind*

In 1996 Daniel Libeskind's 'Spiral', an angular extension planned for the Victoria & Albert Museum (page 82), unfurled a series of rooms and rewound them in a then-shocking way. After many attempts to secure funding and acceptance, it was abandoned in 2004. In the meantime Libeskind's Deconstructivist approach had received acclaim elsewhere, principally in Berlin, easing a return to the British capital with this facility – including teaching spaces, offices and a cafe – for the University's graduate students.

Deconstructing architecture

Libeskind is one of the best known proponents of a mode of architecture that has perhaps done the most to unsettle popular conceptions of how a building should look. Deconstructivism questions the signs and meanings of structures and disassembles and distorts their essentials.

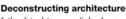

Section

The off-kilter planes and twisted volumes of the Centre are clear in a cross-section. Made up of three parts fantastically conjoined, the dynamism of this fractured geometry has been viewed as appropriate for its busy urban context.

Slanting stair

Deconstructivists sought new interpretations of standard architectural features. Libeskind's main stair alters its angles, walls and ceiling from the norm, encouraging exploration (perhaps unwisely in a place in which young people and alcohol often mix), but retains a purposeful progression up and through the building.

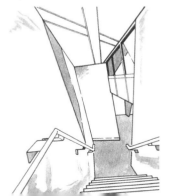

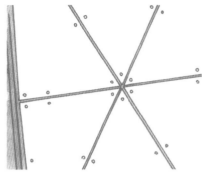

Silver skin

The building's stainless steel cladding was also a departure. Its dull reflectivity and durability were aesthetic and practical in purpose. This was one of a range of new materials appearing at this time; others included titanium, copper and ceramic, which was often coloured.

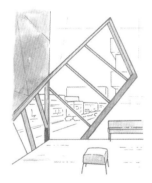

Broken windows

Windows also ceased to follow the rigid Cartesian logic of previous movements, sloping and slashing their way through the façade. They give exciting views into and out of the building, revealing and framing movement and light in new ways.

15½ Consort Road

Location *London SE15*
Date *2003–05*
Architects *Richard Paxton Architects, MOOARC (architects), Flower Michelin (fit-out)*

At the opposite end of the scale to the luxury apartments that tend to characterise London's property market today, the unique character of the capital has continued to see individuals find, secure and exploit the most unpromising of spaces to build one-off homes to live in. Monty Ravenscroft extracted a highly liveable three-bedroom house from a long, irregular plot between two listed period houses and severe planning constraints. Architect-led but a true self build, the project was chosen for the popular television series *Grand Designs*.

Grand design

One stipulation was that the house not be obvious from the street, which was met by placing a screened multi-purpose room between the road and the living area proper. This also ameliorated noise. The cladding is fireproofed phenolic plywood throughout, on composite walls and steel framing.

Cutaway

The elements of the brief are arranged to gain the most space possible. Importantly, bedrooms at either end of the house are raised just enough to clear the typical head height of users in the 'wet' rooms below. This drawing omits the long kitchen and storage bar.

Light saviours

Since no windows were permitted in the sides or front, the three-part sliding glass roof was critical. On a stainless-steel frame and weighing 600 kg (1,320 lb), it opens in seconds to emulate a Roman atrium. Elsewhere, roof lights, mirrors and switchable glass all brighten the house.

Double duty

Most fixtures and fittings perform secondary functions. A retractable television reveals a fireplace, a light fitting is combined with a shower head and a cupboard back can be replaced by a film projector. Panels hide drawers and chutes, a sliding bed and a spa bath.

Garden front

Bi-fold doors show the increased freedom at the back of the plot. The room itself is used for living, sleeping and entertaining. The thermal mass of the part-concrete structure, underfloor warming, a heat exchanger and drawn air act together to condition the interior.

Bankside 123

Location
*Southwark Street
London SE1*
Date *2005–07*
Architects *Allies and
Morrison*

The transformation of the South Bank begun by the Festival of Britain (page 176) has taken many more years than might reasonably have been expected. For centuries a base for activities deemed unsuitable for Westminster and the City, it was until very recently dominated by industry, warehousing and support or back offices for the Square Mile and West End. This is one of the new developments that is at last changing that picture conclusively.

Work/life balance

Improving the public realm – roads, pavements and squares, along with landscaping and street furniture – is now an accepted goal of any new development. Bankside 123 introduces streets between its office blocks, ground-floor retail, paved areas for eating out and a triangular greened space.

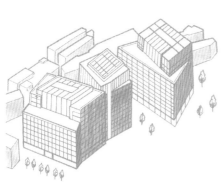

Street scene

Although larger than its predecessors, Bankside 123's permeability and form are a gain. Practising what it preaches Allies and Morrison, based opposite in an eclectic mix of buildings, run a café and have turned a service alley into a small street.

Public or private?

Like a flap bent from a piece of card, a cut into the façade of the phase 1 building eases entrance and is a handy place for passers-by to shelter from the rain. Blurring boundaries is attractive, but gives rise to uncertainty.

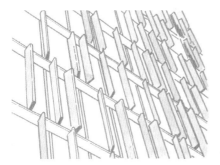

'Blue Fin' building

Above, phase 1 has vertical aluminium slats to shade its glazed elevations and for visual interest, hence its nickname. Terracotta is used on the later buildings 2 and 3. All these panels were safely installed from the inside by powered manipulator, a quiet improvement in construction technology.

In and out

Each of the buildings is asymmetric internally and externally. Atriums, widespread since the 1980s, are central or pushed to one side, to give flexibility for occupiers in what was a speculative scheme. Upper-floor outside terraces, also common, are another tenant amenity.

Chobham Academy

Location *Cheering Lane London E20*
Date *2004–12*
Architect *AHMM*

School daze
A circular plan for the middle and upper building closed an axial vista, addressed the established and new halves of the site and was neither more expensive nor less practical than a more conventional shape. The school's specialism is literature and the performing arts.

This new academy school was conceived before the formal award of the 2012 summer Olympic Games to London, as part of major regeneration of its Stratford neighbourhood. Its collection of vigorous volumes, centred on a drum, makes a strong architectural statement amidst the box-like blocks of the former Olympic Village, legacy of an early decision to have occasional incident amongst grids of repetitive housing. Crisp cladding and tough concrete shelter straightforward, robust and low-maintenance teaching spaces.

Making an entrance

The specialist building contains a sports hall, dance and drama studios and a 'black box' theatre with exposed services and retractable seating. Saw-tooth roof lights service art and design technology rooms and an atrium. Ribbed concrete facing was acid-etched to highlight the aggregate's mica.

Growing up

The rectilinear lower block provides efficient, changeable rooms for infants and a nursery (with 'Olympic Ring' porthole windows). Coloured vestibule walls particular to each block enable pupils to track their advancement through the years. A landscaped semi-public realm knits the buildings together.

Clever cladding

Opening windows were thought inadvisable due to noise, so the distinctive nozzles within the cladding system for the two main blocks draw in air that is acoustically damped over baffles and heated. A high flow of air is maintained to ensure alertness in class.

Drum role

Divided by a galleried atrium into open and more private areas, the drum's projecting 'lobes' hold fully serviced rooms. Their glass and spandrel panels incline at opposing angles. Glulam (glued, laminated) timber beams support a polymer pillow roof, on which there are open teaching terraces.

London Aquatics Centre

Location *Olympic Park London E20*

Date *2005–11*

Architects *Zaha Hadid Architects (architects), Arup (engineers)*

As with the nearby Chobham Academy (page 242), the Centre began before London 2012. Its form was inspired by water in motion. A smooth concrete podium or base, necessary because of infrastructure and public access, works at ground level, supports pre-cast concrete terraces covered by the spectacular organic form of an aluminium-clad roof that requires no internal columns to hold it up, ensuring clear views for all. A warm-up pool within the podium is top-lit through geometric gaps punched in the concrete.

Liquidity

Shorn of the crude 'water wings' of additional seating installed for the Olympics, Hadid's free-form approach became much clearer. The immaculately-poured concrete is left unfinished, emphasising its unique nature, and the shell-like form appears to float above its podium.

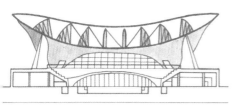

Sinuous section

The sweeping steel roof is made from parallel fan trusses almost 12 m (40 ft) deep at its centre yet its edges, above the glazed side walls, are thin and light enough to be self-supporting. Fixed at two points, it rests on bearings at a third.

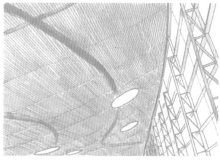

Meeting of materials

The underside of the roof is lined with thin strips of Brazilian hardwood, stained grey and fixed to more sustainable timber backing. The great glass façades that replaced the temporary seating are braced with aluminium trusses and frames.

Concrete curves

The plasticity of concrete as a medium is often demonstrated. Here it resolves the junctions of a glazed wall that is canted and also curved in more than one plane, another with a simple concavity and a corridor bowed in plan.

Diving detail

The fluid lines that inform the Centre are carried through every detail; the rigid diving platforms, for example, though made of concrete, bend over the water as if to drink. They are also evocative of inter-war work in this material in France and Belgium.

Saw Swee Hock Student Centre

Location *Sheffield Street London WC2*

Date *2009–14*

Architects *O'Donnell + Twomey*

The world-renowned London School of Economics has been steadily expanding its tightly-knitted campus north of the Strand for over a century. Named in honour of an LSE alumnus and statistics professor, this is the new locus for its student body. A large basement events space can be seen from the street where it rises to triple height; a ground-floor pub seems well-placed. On the upper storeys a cafe, multifaith centre, Students' Union offices, gym, careers office and terraces can be found. The Centre is also a shop window for the LSE.

Open doors
The folded façades extrude the site's jagged street pattern upward. They also create pockets of public space along the pavement and invite people into the building by leading both the eye and the foot inward. The brick finish settles the newcomer into its surroundings.

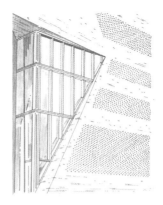

Progressive plan

Privacy versus openness, solid or transparent, lit and dark, small as opposed to large: the many, sometimes quite major, functional differences at each level required similarly differing structural, service and elevational treatments. The sloped brick plane is intersected. The main stair connects all.

Cut-outs

The inclination of the walls was driven partly by compliance with rights of light. The diagonal fenestration complements this, as do the passages of open-work brick where regular gaps are left by offsetting. Glazed behind, they allow daylight in and artificial light out.

Spiral stair

A wide stair in bare concrete makes a tight spiral up through the building, wrapping around the lift shafts. Landing locations and shapes vary, depending on the needs of the floor, but movement is continuous, animating the Centre with its users.

Bonding over brick

This traditional London material is adapted for today's more energetic architecture by its orientation, spacing and participation in the lighting scheme. The perforated sections are linked to the concrete structure for stability. The 'special' bricks used were carefully plotted.

Location Map

As the century drew to a close, London continued to witness new architectures and new civic projects, whether the Lloyd's building or the Sainsbury Wing or the British Library. The rejuvenation of Dockland and the celebration of the millennium coincided, shifting energies toward the eastern edge of the capital, while the south bank of the river finally became a third area of decisive focus for the future.

1 Lloyd's of London
Lime Street, EC3
page 210

2 British Library
Euston Road, NW1
page 212

3 Broadgate & Finsbury Avenue
Liverpool Street, EC3
page 214

4 Cascades
Westferry Road, E14
page 216

5 National Gallery Sainsbury Wing
Trafalgar Square, WC2
page 218

6 No. 1 Poultry
EC2 *page 220*

7 Canary Wharf
West India Avenue, E14 *page 222*

8 Millennium Dome
Peninsular Square, SE10 *page 224*

9 30 St Mary Axe
EC3 *page 226*

10 Peckham Library
Peckham Hill Street, SE15 *page 228*

11 Southwark underground station
Blackfriars Road SE1
page 230

12 The Shard
London Bridge Street, SE1 *page 232*

13 Maggie's West London
Charing Cross Hospital
Fulham Palace Road, W6 *page 234*

14 Graduate Centre, London Metropolitan University
Holloway Road, N7
page 236

Hyde Park

W6

Ba

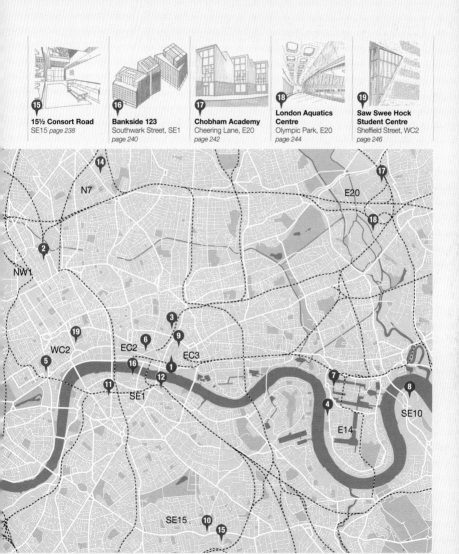

15 **15½ Consort Road**
SE15 *page 238*

16 **Bankside 123**
Southwark Street, SE1
page 240

17 **Chobham Academy**
Cheering Lane, E20
page 242

18 **London Aquatics Centre**
Olympic Park, E20
page 244

19 **Saw Swee Hock Student Centre**
Sheffield Street, WC2
page 246

N7

NW1

WC2

EC2

EC3

SE1

E20

E14

SE10

SE15

249

Prominent Architects

CHARLES BARRY

Bridgewater House (page 76)

Palace of Westminster
(page 74)

FOSTER + PARTNERS

30 St Mary Axe (page 226)

Broadgate and Finsbury Avenue
(page 214)

Canary Wharf (page 222)

City Hall

Great Court at the British
Museum

Imperial War Museum

Principal Tower

JAMES GIBBS

St Martin-in-the-Fields
(page 42)

St Mary le Strand (page 32)

ZAHA HADID

Evelyn Grace Academy

London Aquatics Centre
(page 244)

Serpentine Sackler Gallery

NICHOLAS HAWKSMOOR

Christ Church, Spitalfields
(page 34)

St George, Bloomsbury
(page 40)

CHARLES HOLDEN

55 Broadway (page 152)

Senate House (page 162)

DENYS LASDUN

26 St James's Place (page 188)

Institute of Education
(page 202)

National Theatre (page 198)

Royal College of Physicians
(page 190)

ROBERT MATTHEW

New Zealand House (page 184)

Royal Festival Hall (page 176)

JOHN NASH

Park Village West and Park
Village East (page 66)

The Nash Route (page 60)

RENZO PIANO

The Shard (page 232)

RICHARD ROGERS

88 Wood Street

The Leadenhall Building

Lloyd's of London (page 210)

Millennium Dome (page 224)

GEORGE GILBERT SCOTT

Midland Grand Hotel (page 90)

Public Offices (page 84)

SKIDMORE, OWINGS & MERRILL

Baltimore Tower

Broadgate and Finsbury Avenue
(page 214)

Canary Wharf (page 222)

CHRISTOPHER WREN

Royal Hospital, Chelsea
(page 24)

Royal Hospital for Seamen
(page 26)

Kensington Palace (page 28)

St Paul's Cathedral (page 20)

St Stephen Walbrook (page 22)

Resources

Architectural Styles – A Visual Guide
by Owen Hopkins
(Laurence King, 2014)

The Buildings of England: London
(six volumes) by various authors
(Penguin/Yale University Press, 1983–2005)

Guide to the Architecture of London
by Edward Jones, Christopher Woodward
(W&N, 2013)

London Heritage: The Changing Style of a City
by Michael Jenner
(Michael Joseph, 1988)

*New City: Contemporary Architecture in the
City of London*
by Alec Forshaw
(Merrell, 2013)

Underground Architecture
by David Lawrence
(Capital Transport, 1994)

Glossary

ARCADE A series of arches resting on columns or piers.

AREA A void in the pavement lighting a basement, usually with stairs down.

ART DECO Inter-war decorative style of geometry and clean lines named after a Paris exposition of 1925.

ART NOUVEAU Continental European style of decoration and architecture from the end of the 19th century using plant-like, organic forms.

ARTS AND CRAFTS British design movement of the late 19th century inspired by an idealised medieval past.

ATRIUM Circulation space occupying the full height of a building; open to the sky (historic) or glazed over (post-c.1850).

BALUSTER/BALUSTRADE Individual/a group of vertical supports for a staircase handrail.

BAROQUE Theatrical style of continental European architecture and interior design popularised in Britain from the late 17th century.

BAS-RELIEF Shallowly cut carving common on inter-war buildings.

BAY Projecting part of a façade beginning at ground floor; rhythmic, vertical subdivision of a façade.

BEAUX-ARTS Style of late 19th-century civic architecture characterised by symmetry and grandeur. From the French arts school.

BLIND (of a window) Not fully penetrating the wall and therefore unglazed.

BRUTALISM *See* New Brutalism.

CANTILEVER Element that projects horizontally beyond its closest visible support.

CHICAGO SCHOOL American architectural movement from the late 19th century focused on tall, steel-framed commercial buildings with large windows and minimal decoration.

CLASSICAL Architectural style drawn from ancient Greek and Roman principles of building.

CLERESTORY Thin strip of glazing at the top of a wall.

COFFER Recessed part of a ceiling, usually encountered in multiples, arranged as a pattern.

COLONNADE Run of columns used to define a space inside or outside.

COMPOSITE Classical column order whose capital combines elements of the Corinthian and Ionic.

CORINTHIAN Classical column order with elaborate foliage on its capital.

CORNICE Moulding across the top of a façade, used as its visual termination.

CORPORATE MODERNISM Post-war American architectural style of glazed, highly serviced buildings, often for commercial firms.

CURTAIN WALL Modernist, non-structural cladding of glass, 'hung' against the structure like a curtain.

DECONSTRUCTIVISM Late 20th-century architectural movement that questions and breaks down conventional architectural elements.

DORIC Classical column order with plain capital; *see also* Tuscan.

ENTABLATURE Horizontal element connecting the tops of columns or pilasters.

FENESTRATION The pattern and shape of the window openings in a façade.

GIANT-ORDER Columns that extend through more than one storey.

GOTHIC Originating in medieval France, an architectural and decorative style using pointed arches, carving and verticality.

HIGH TECH Broadly British post-war architectural movement stressing technology and flexibility.

INTERNATIONAL STYLE Severe, minimalist interpretation of inter-war architectural Modernism.

IONIC Classical column order with two or more scrolls for its capital.

LANTERN Raised, glazed area in a roof admitting light.

LOGGIA An open-air space comprising a run of columns and a roof.

MANNERISM Individualised version of another period or style, such as Baroque.

MASSING How a building occupies the volume it fills, e.g. a single tower, two low wings.

MEGASTRUCTURE Very large building, often of bare concrete, containing multiple functions within its flexible interior.

MODERNE Streamlined, more populist branch of inter-war architectural Modernism.

MODERNISM Overarching cultural movement originating in Europe in the 1920s that rejected ornament and embraced functionality.

MULLION Vertical or horizontal framing element of a window.

NEW BRUTALISM Post-war architectural style often using bare concrete. From *béton brut*, the French for raw concrete.

OCULUS Circular opening, which may be glazed or left open.

ORIEL Bay that begins above the ground floor.

PALAZZO Medieval Italian building form with strong horizontal layers; originally described a palace, later and more commonly an urban house.

PALLADIANISM English architectural style of the early 18th century paying tribute to Roman Classicism.

PARAMETRIC Design methodology using complex computing to manipulate parameters to achieve a solution.

PAVILION Small, free-standing building for occasional or temporary use or element of a larger building designed to appear as such.

PEDIMENT Triangular or rounded Classical element above an entablature and usually supported on columns.

PERISTYLE Circular colonnade.

PERPENDICULAR Form of Gothic architecture with vertically oriented tracery.

PIANO NOBILE Floor containing the principal rooms of a private house or public venue; from the Italian for noble storey.

PILASTER A column sliced lengthways and set against a wall.

PILOTIS Columns supporting, or appearing to support, all or part of a building. From the French for piers.

PORTICO Projecting entrance.

POSTMODERNISM Post-war style of architecture and design that deliberately and often humorously subverts Classical motifs.

QUEEN ANNE STYLE A mix of old English and northern European architectural motifs from late 19th-century English design.

QUOIN Decorative piece for an exterior corner.

RENAISSANCE Sixteenth-century artistic rebirth in continental Europe; architectural style of that time.

RUSTICATION Decorative treatment applied to the lower part of a façade. May be channelled, pillowed, etc.

SEGMENTAL Rounded.

SERVICE CORE Clustered lifts, staircases and ducting for wires and pipes, usually within a concrete structural shaft.

SPANDREL Space between arches or an arch and its surround; panel below the glazed part of a window.

STRING COURSE Thin, specially emphasised horizontal band of brick or stone in a façade.

TUSCAN Classical column order with plain capital; *see also* Doric.

TYMPANUM Space immediately above an entrance, often semicircular.

VENETIAN WINDOW A tall, round-headed light flanked by shorter, square-topped lights in a single composition.

Index

Acknowledgements

Author Acknowledgement
Thanks to the Ivy Press team again, principally Tom Kitch, Jamie Pumfrey and Caroline Earle, and especially for the chance to write about my home city. This book is dedicated to another Londoner, my mother.

The publisher would like to thank the following for permission to reproduce copyright material:

Alamy/ Aardvark: 58; Matthew Chattle: 56; A.P.S. (UK): 48; Archimage: 242; DBURKE: 236; Angelo Hornak: 26, 122; carol moir: 144–5; mark phillips: 106; robertharding: 210; Marcin Rogozinski: 98; Travelpix: 24; VIEW Pictures Ltd: 140.

Drapers' Company: © The Drapers' Company of the City of London: 92.

Getty/ Heritage Images: 20.

James Lawrence: 2, 14, 22, 30, 40, 44, 60, 66, 76, 78, 86, 96, 102, 108, 118, 128, 132, 134, 146, 150, 152, 154, 156, 164, 166, 168, 174, 178, 180, 184, 186, 196, 200, 202, 228, 232, 238, 240.

Jamie Barras: 188.

Shutterstock/ alessandro0770: 52; Tony Baggett: 80, 116; Baloncici: 34; BasPhoto: 126, 158; Philip Bird LRPS CPAGB: 136; Dan Breckwoldt: 226; Byjeng: 130; chrisdorney: 82; Paul Daniels: 114–15; Claudio Divizia: 16, 42, 50, 64, 172–3, 176, 190, 198, 204, 220,

230; Ron Ellis: 160, 212, 234, 246; Eterovic: 74; e X p o s e: 244; Stephen Finn: 10–11, 100; fritz16: 94, 120; Zoltan Gabor: 148; godrick: 12, 68; Botond Horvath: 54; ileana_bt: 218; jennyt: 162; JJFarq: 84; Pawell Libera: 6–7; LTerlecka: 124; Igor Matic: 32; Iain McGillivray: 192; mikecphoto: 194; Anna Moskvina: 62; Sailesh Patel: 222; pcruciatti: 104; William Perugini: 232; r.nagy: 208–9; Alexandre Rotenberg: 214; Samot: 72–3; Pete Spiro: 90; IR Stone: 138; TTstudio: 110; Tupungato: 182; Simonas Vaikasas: 216; vichie81: 4–5; Kiev.Victor: 18, 38–9, 46, 88; Cedric Weber: 28; yampi: 224.